Praise for
such a pretty picture

"In this courageous survival story of harrowing sexual abuse, relentless gaslighting, and temporary silencing, a father's dark psychology and a mother's literal and figurative blindness meet one small girl's unshakeable will to endure. If you know a survivor of childhood predation, (and trust me, you do) this book, so full of candor and bravery and language's redemptive lyric flight, will be a talisman for healing."

—PAM HOUSTON,
author of *Deep Creek: Finding Hope in the High Country*

"Leeb has written my favorite kind of memoir: frantically alive, unflinching, breaking my heart in the best ways. I felt her with me on every page, and by Chapter Three, we were best friends."

—JOSHUA MOHR, author of *Model Citizen*

"*Such a Pretty Picture* was raw and aching, but impossible to look away from. . . . one of the most honest, powerful memoirs I've ever read. Andrea Leeb isn't asking for pity. She's telling her story to shed light, to speak the truth, and to make someone else feel less alone. And that's precisely why it matters."

—*LOS ANGELES BOOK REVIEW*, 5-star review

"Startling emotional rawness. Unflinching truth-telling. Andrea Leeb's devastating examination of a childhood shattered by parental sexual and emotional abuse will be seared into your mind from the very first page. The immediacy of Leeb's propulsive writing rivets your attention, but it is her bravery to not just survive but also make a beautiful life that gives this story such resonance. Wrenching, unforgettable, and, ultimately, illuminating, *Such a Pretty Picture* carried my heart away."

—SAMANTHA DUNN,
author of *Not by Accident: Reconstructing a Careless Life*

"It's a story about survival—of trauma, betrayal, and, surprisingly, moments of love—rendered with a clarity that's both poetic and emotionally searing."

—SEATTLE BOOK REVIEW, 5-star review

"Andrea Leeb's debut memoir recounts in stunning detail the devastating story of how a daughter's secret and a family's betrayal carved the way forward for a resilient young woman determined to survive. This work is full of beautifully rendered, thought-provoking prose that ultimately uplifts as it inspires."

—ELLE JOHNSON, author of *The Officer's Daughter* and executive producer of *Bosch*

"With crystalline prose and a measured, evocative tone, Leeb guides the reader through her childhood in a home that, from the outside, appeared perfect—but behind closed doors, hid deep dysfunction."

—SAN DIEGO BOOK REVIEW, 5-star review

"*Such a Pretty Picture* is a fierce act of reclamation, written with haunting grace. Brave, honest, and exquisitely written, this memoir is a necessary addition to the canon of survival literature. Leeb's story will stay with readers long after the final page."

—PORTLAND BOOK REVIEW, 5-star review

"Andrea Leeb's powerful memoir *Such a Pretty Picture* is an immensely compelling, tender, honest, and ultimately courageous reckoning with abuse, betrayal, and the false promises of new starts. She writes with great immediacy and clarity about the long, often seemingly impossible, and always mysterious journey into a lifetime of unfolding healing."

—CARYN MIRRIAM-GOLDBERG, Kansas Poet Laureate Emeritus and author of *The Magic Eye: A Memoir of Saving a Life and Place in the Age of Anxiety*

". . . With exquisite writing, Andrea bravely explores the wounds that shaped her and the healing that comes from confronting her past."

—WENDY ADAMSON, author of *Mother Load*

such a pretty picture

A Memoir

Andrea Leeb

SHE WRITES PRESS

Copyright © 2025 Andrea Leeb

All rights reserved. No part of this publication may be reproduced, stored in a retrieval system, or transmitted in any form or by any means, electronic, mechanical, photocopying, recording, or otherwise, except for brief quotations in reviews, educational works, or other uses permitted by copyright law.

Published in 2025 by
She Writes Press, an imprint of The Stable Book Group

32 Court Street, Suite 2109
Brooklyn, NY 11201
https://shewritespress.com

Library of Congress Control Number: 2025910537
ISBN: 978-1-64742-994-2
e-ISBN: 978-1-64742-995-9

Interior designer: Katherine Lloyd, The DESK

Printed in the United States

Names and identifying characteristics have been changed to protect the privacy of certain individuals.

No part of this publication may be used to train generative artificial intelligence (AI) models. The publisher and author reserve all rights related to the use of this content in machine learning.

All company and product names mentioned in this book may be trademarks or registered trademarks of their respective owners. They are used for identification purposes only and do not imply endorsement or affiliation.

For Sarai

author's note

This is a work of nonfiction. The events and experiences herein are true and reflect my recollection to the best of my ability. Except for the names of my immediate family, all of the names and some identifying details and locations have been changed in order to respect and protect the privacy of others.

Part One
1962-1969

chapter 1

It began the first time my father gave me a bath. That night, a Saturday in late September 1962, my parents had plans to meet friends for dinner in Manhattan. "A date," my mother said, even though they were already married.

I stood in the bedroom I shared with my sister, Sarai, watching my mother slip a pair of footed pajamas over her feet. Once my mother finished with her, it would be time for my nightly bath. My favorite part of the day, and the only time I knew for certain I would get my mother's undivided attention.

"Andrea," my mother said after she tucked Sarai into her crib, "I asked Daddy to give you a bath while I get ready." She petted the top of my head.

Hiding my disappointment, I forced a smile. My mother seemed so excited. We lived in an apartment in Queens. Although my mother loved Manhattan—the real city, she called it—she rarely went there. When she did, she always had me, age four and a half, and two-year-old Sarai in tow.

"Daddy wants to give me a bath?" I bit my lower lip.

My father, who taught English at a local high school and went to graduate school at night, was hardly ever home before I went to bed. On the few nights he came home early, he sat alone in the living room listening to records or reading thick books and drinking from glasses filled with ice and a clear liquid that looked like water, but was called gin.

such a pretty picture

My mother laughed. "Of course, he does. Daddy loves you."

Taking my hand, she led me into the bathroom. Dressed in a freshly pressed white T-shirt and boxer shorts—my mother ironed all of our clothing, even our underwear—my father stood in front of the sink. He turned and smiled at us. Tall and dark, my father had straight white teeth and a wide smile. If not for a chip on one of his front teeth, his smile would've been perfect.

"Be a good girl for Daddy," my mother said, giving my hand to my father as if I were a gift.

Alone, my father and I stared at each other.

"Come on, cutie. Let's get this bath going."

I undressed while my father ran the water. I watched him adjust the knobs and stick his hand under the faucet.

"Tell me if the temperature is okay for you," he said once the bathtub had filled.

Naked, I bent down and stuck my hand into the water. It felt warm but not too warm.

"Good," I said.

"Remember to speak in sentences. It is good."

"It is good," I repeated.

"That's my smart girl." My father picked me up and pressed my body against his chest. He smelled like limes and laundry detergent. His freshly shaved face felt smooth.

He had a dot of shaving cream on one side of his face. "You missed a spot." I put my finger on the dot.

My father laughed, gave me a sloppy kiss, and lowered me into the tub. "I almost forgot your duck." He grabbed a yellow rubber duck off the bathroom shelf. The duck was Sarai's, not mine; I considered myself too old for a rubber duck. But happy for his attention, I took it.

My mother had left a pink washcloth on the edge of the tub. I soaked it and rubbed it with soap, just like she'd taught me. I stuck my head under the water, then scrubbed my face and my neck with the washcloth. My father knelt next to the bathtub. I couldn't see his hands or his legs, but he seemed to be squirming.

"Daddy?"

His eyes met mine. "Play with your duck, and let Daddy wash you with his hand." He reached into the bathtub and took my washcloth away from me. "Doesn't that feel nice," he said, running a hand over my body.

I didn't answer him. He rubbed my neck, my chest, my legs, and then the place in between. He didn't use soap, and he used only one hand. His breathing grew fast and heavy.

"The water's getting cold," I said. It was a lie, but my father's breathing scared me. The way he touched me felt strange: good but not good.

He didn't respond, so I said his name again, louder this time. I slid closer to the wall to get out of his reach. I wanted to stand up. To jump out of the tub.

I heard the click of my mother's heels before I saw her. Petite and delicate, my mother had thick mink-brown hair, porcelain skin, and sharp, fine features with high apple-shaped cheekbones. Everyone said she looked like a movie star. She hadn't finished getting ready, and wore only a full black slip, sheer black stockings, and high heels.

"David, what is taking so . . ." She didn't finish her sentence. "Oh my God, what are you doing?"

My father jerked his hand away from me. He bent down slightly and yanked the waist of his boxer shorts. He scrunched up his face. I couldn't tell if he was angry or scared. Or both.

"David!" My mother's voice sounded the way it did when she thought I was about to run into traffic.

My father stood up and, as he turned to face her, she screamed again. A scream without words; sharp and shrill, more like a howl than a scream. I'd never heard anyone scream like that.

such a pretty picture

Too afraid to move, I clutched the duck. Suddenly, my mother's legs went out from under her. She crumpled like a paper doll. My father caught her before her head hit the tile floor.

"Mommy!" I screamed. "What's wrong with Mommy?" I started to cry.

"Shut up and get out of the goddamned tub." Kneeling on the floor, my father held my mother's limp body against his chest. He was so big and she was so small; she looked like a child in his arms. "Marlene, wake up. Please wake up."

My legs wobbled as I climbed out of the tub. I wanted to throw up. Looking at my mother lying in my father's arms, I thought she was dead. I thought we had killed her.

"David," she whispered after a few seconds.

Hearing her voice, my tears came faster. "Mommy." I wanted to go to her, but my father blocked me with a hand.

"David, I can't see anything," she said, her voice growing louder. "I'm blind."

chapter 2

Naked and wet, I followed my father as he carried my mother from the bathroom into their bedroom.

My father lowered my mother onto the edge of their bed. "I can't see," she said.

"It's all right, sweetheart," he said, stroking her hair. "I'm here."

My mother had been planning to wear her good black dress. Still on its hanger, the dress was laid across the center of their bed.

"I'll help you get dressed," he said. "Everything is going to be fine."

He slipped the dress over her head and helped her put her arms through the holes. I stood against the wall, watching. Goose bumps covered my naked body. I could hear Sarai crying for our mother but everyone ignored her.

"Almost done," my father said. The dress had tiny pearl buttons down the back, and he carefully buttoned each one. When he finished, my father looked over at me and scowled.

"What are you doing standing there?"

"Is Mommy okay?"

"Your sister's crying. Go check on her. And for God's sake, put on a nightgown."

In our bedroom, Sarai stood in her crib with her fingers wrapped around the bars. Tears ran down her face. She had thrown Puppy, the stuffed dog she slept with, onto the floor.

such a pretty picture

I picked it up and handed it to her. "Poor Puppy," I said, trying to make my voice sound soothing.

"No!" She threw it back over the bars. "I want Mommy."

Normally, I would have tried to comfort her. I might even have climbed into her crib but not this time. All I cared about was getting back to my mother.

My mother had left my nightgown on my bed. I fingered the soft flannel and the pink ribbon at the neck. Earlier, I'd watched her as she took it out of my dresser. Humming to herself, she'd put it on my bed and smoothed it out flat with her hands. She seemed so happy then. Now, as I wriggled into it, I remembered the look on her face and the sound of her scream after she walked into the bathroom. I started to cry again.

I found my parents in the living room. My mother sat on the couch. She reminded me of one of the glass figurines she kept on a shelf in her bedroom: beautiful but too delicate to touch.

My father paced back and forth in front of her. He was frowning, and as he paced, he clenched and unclenched his fists. Our TV was directly across from the couch, and I positioned myself in front of it—close enough for me to watch my mother, without getting in the way of my father's pacing.

"Mommy, you look so pretty," I smiled at her. I expected her to smile back. When she didn't, I felt a prick in my chest. I held my breath so I wouldn't cry again, but a stream of tears came anyway. Afraid that my father would notice, I wiped my face with the sleeve of my nightgown. "Are you still going out to dinner?"

"Don't be stupid," my father snapped. "I'm taking her to the hospital."

"Mommy!" Sarai shrieked from our bedroom.

My mother stood up but my father put his hand on her arm, easing her back onto the couch.

"I told you to take care of your sister," he said to me.

"She wants Mommy, not me."

"David, go get her," my mother said firmly.

"Andrea can watch her," he said. "She'll settle down and cry herself to sleep. You need to rest until the sitter gets here."

"I want her. Bring her to me."

My father shook his head and then shot me a dark look. "Don't bother your mother."

Once he left, I sat down next to her, inhaling the scent of her gardenia perfume. "I love you, Mommy." I took her hand.

She pulled it away. "Not now, Andrea."

I covered my face with my hands and shut my eyes. I didn't open them until my father came back carrying my sister a few minutes later.

He put her down on the other side of my mother. Still crying, she crawled onto my mother's lap. I watched as my mother ran her fingers through Sarai's golden curls. Even without seeing, she twisted them into tiny perfect ringlets, as if she had memorized each hair on my sister's head.

"Andrea, I need to talk to you." My father motioned for me to follow him into the hallway.

He bent down next to me and took my shoulders between his big hands. "What happened tonight is your fault."

"I'm sorry," I said, unsure about what I'd done wrong.

"If you want Mommy to get better, you can't tell anyone what happened. This has to be our secret. Forever."

chapter 3

I was too young to fully understand what happened in the bathroom, but on some subconscious level I understood that my childhood had changed. My parents and I became keepers of a shared secret.

My mother spent two weeks at a hospital in Manhattan. I'd never know for certain if it was a general hospital or a psychiatric hospital, although I always suspected the latter. Later I learned that my mother had been diagnosed with hysterical blindness. A diagnosis that would forever remind me of something out of a Greek tragedy or nineteenth-century novel. To put it simply, hysterical blindness is a rare neurological reaction triggered by stress. In the hospital and for the next sixty years my mother explained the incident away: "I walked into the bathroom and saw my husband bathing my daughter in cold water. I went crazy." As far as I know, no one ever questioned her story.

While my mother was away, my father stayed with a friend who lived near the hospital and Nanny, my mother's mother, came to take care of Sarai and me. I loved Nanny, but I missed my mother, and I was terrified that she was never coming back.

A soft, plump woman with thick brown hair, Nanny wore cotton housedresses with silver snaps and deep pockets bulging with butterscotch candies and tissues. She had a double chin and a longish nose. My mother had her smile and her hair, but other than that I didn't think they looked anything alike. It made me glad I looked more like my mother than Nanny, but—although I hated to admit it—with my olive skin, puffy lips, and dark narrow eyes, I resembled my father most of all.

At our apartment, Nanny slept on the foldout couch in our living room. She could have stayed in my parents' room, but she didn't want to. "I want to keep it nice for when Mommy comes back," she said.

I tried my best to be good for Nanny, especially because Sarai screamed for my mother constantly. "She's a toddler, it's not her fault," Nanny explained to me when I pointed it out. "But you have to be brave." Each time she told me that I'd nod, but I envied Sarai. I wanted to cry. I wanted to lie down, kick my feet, and pound my fists against the floor. But more importantly, I wanted to tell my grandmother what happened in the bathroom. I wanted to crawl into her arms and confess to her that it was my fault my mother had gone blind. Several times, I came close, but then, remembering my father's admonition, I'd feel my throat close before I could form the words.

"Is Mommy really here?" I asked my grandmother. I'd just gotten home from preschool, and we stood together in front of my parents' closed bedroom door.

"She's home but she is still blind." Nanny knelt next to me, putting her hands on my shoulders. She stroked my hair. "Do you remember what blind means?"

I shuddered, recalling the night in the bathroom. "Mommy can't see me," I said. "But I can see her? Hug her?" I hoped that if my mother held me and I held her, she'd know how sorry I was. Maybe if she knew, she'd want to see me again. Maybe I could cure her with my love, the same way I had hurt her with my badness.

"You can sit on her lap, but you need to sit very still."

such a pretty picture

"Can I see her now?" I wiggled away from Nanny and hopped from one foot to the other.

My grandmother put a finger to her lips. Then taking my hand, she opened the door.

My mother sat on a purple velvet chair with gold legs. Dressed in a silky cream robe trimmed with lace, she reminded me of a fairy-tale princess. I wanted to run to her, throw myself on top of her, but my grandmother wouldn't let go of my hand. A bouquet of yellow roses had been placed on the dresser and a vase filled with gardenias on the nightstand. The bedroom smelled sweet and fresh like a mixture of flowers and talcum powder.

Sarai napped in her playpen next to my mother's chair and a wave of jealousy hit me. Why did Sarai get to see our mother first? I almost started to whine about it, but then I noticed my father sitting on the edge of the bed. I hadn't seen him since he'd taken my mother to the hospital. He stood up and I squeezed my grandmother's hand.

"Hi, cutie," he said and bent down to pick me up. "Remember, our secret," he whispered, pressing his lips against my ear.

Hearing him, my stomach cramped, but only for a second. The moment he lowered me onto my mother's lap, I forgot everything and everyone else.

"Mommy!" I squealed.

"Be still," my grandmother said.

But I couldn't. I threw my arms around her and hugged her. "I missed you so much." I buried my face in her neck. Inhaling her smell, I wanted to stay with her forever.

"I missed you too," she said, but her voice sounded like she was far away.

Trying to get her attention, I snuggled deeper into her body. "I love you, Mommy."

I wanted her to stroke my hair, to kiss me and feel my face with her fingers. But she sat with her arms at her side, refusing to touch me. I felt like crying, but I knew if I did everyone would get angry.

I was on her lap for only a few minutes before she pushed me away.

"I'm tired, I have to lie down," she said.

"But I just . . ."

"Let's all go play in your room," my grandmother said, picking up Sarai.

Head down, I walked toward the door.

"Andrea," my mother called after me.

I turned, barely able to stop myself from running back to her. "Mommy?"

"Be a good girl for your father. Do whatever he tells you." She stared at me through eyes that couldn't see.

chapter 4

I knew my mother was afraid, and in the weeks that she stayed blind I tried to make her feel better. Every night I'd offer to read her a story. Every night she refused me. I'd sit alone in my room with an open book. Too upset to read, I'd cry, and as my teardrops splattered onto the pages, I'd pray for my mother to change her mind. I wanted her to hold me close again and love me the way she had before the bath. But most of all I wanted her to forgive me.

My mother's rejection hurt me in ways I didn't yet have the words to describe. It was my mother who'd taught me to read, and she often told me the story of how I learned. "As soon as I brought you home, I began to read to you," she'd say. "You were only two when you started to mimic me. I'd read a word and then you'd repeat it. Before I knew it you were repeating whole sentences. Then one day, out of the blue, you opened a brand-new book, one we had never read before, and read two whole sentences by yourself. Not a single mistake. I couldn't believe it." I loved that story, and although I didn't remember any of it, as she talked, I'd imagine my two-year-old self sitting with my mother as I repeated and then read words for the first time. I'd see her kissing me and holding me close while I read.

I wasn't home the morning my mother got her sight back, but later that day she came with my grandmother to pick me up at school. By then she had been blind for over a month. It was almost Halloween and our school windows and doors were decorated with paper cutouts of witches, pumpkins, and ghosts. She stood dressed in black capri pants and a red leather jacket with a fox trim collar. The sky was cloudy and gray, but my mother wore a pair of black cat-eye sunglasses. Sarai was in her stroller and Nanny stood next to her.

"Mommy!" I ran to my mother, but afraid to touch her without permission, I stopped a few inches in front of her.

My mother took a step forward and reached for me. "My beautiful girl, let me see you." She pushed up her sunglasses. Our eyes met and we both began to cry.

That night she let me read to her. My father had a class and Nanny was bathing Sarai, so it was just the two of us. I read her a story called "Sweet Porridge," a Grimm's fairy tale about a girl who finds a magic porridge-making pot. After I finished, she clapped and pulled me close just like she used to. Inhaling the scent of her gardenia perfume, I wanted her to hold me like that forever.

Nanny stayed with us for another week. "To help Mommy adjust," she said. After she left, as we settled back into being a family, I hoped things would go back to normal. Most did. My mother cooked, cleaned, shopped, and took care of me and my sister. From the outside everything seemed the same. But something about the way my mother treated me had shifted. She didn't yell at me or hit me, but she acted like she didn't want me around. And although I tried, she never let me read to her again. The harder I tried to get her to love me, the more she rejected me.

In June, seven months after my mother got her sight back, eight months after the bath, my father got a job teaching at a college on Long Island. His new job, along with the extra salary he made by continuing to coach high school football, gave my parents enough money to buy a house in Commack, Long Island.

such a pretty picture

The one-story pale green house was surrounded by other almost identical pastel-colored houses. It had a grassy front yard with a pussy willow tree. In back there was more grass, a patio, a swing set, and a cluster of sweet-smelling lilac bushes. It would be, my mother told me, like having a private playground. The house had three bedrooms and a small den for my father to use as his study. Sarai and I would each get our own bedroom. While the idea of having my own room made me happy, it also scared me. I had shared a room with Sarai since I was three. Even though I still thought of her as a baby, having her in my room made me feel safe.

Before we moved, my father took my mother shopping. They bought new furniture for every room. My parents furnished my and my sister's rooms exactly alike: cream-colored dressers and nightstands decorated with pastel flowers and gold-leaf trim. The flowers were hand-painted in Italy. Our twin beds had pale pink wrought iron frames with tiny wrought iron rosebuds. I thought the dressers and nightstands were too grown up, but the rosebud bed reminded me of Sleeping Beauty. I loved it immediately.

Everything in the house smelled clean and new. The day we moved in, my parents, who had both grown up in apartments, were as giddy as children.

"You girls are so lucky." My mother stood in the kitchen with my father unpacking our dishes. Sarai and I sat on the white linoleum floor a few feet away from them, playing with my dolls. "You get to grow up in a house. I'm twenty-five, and this is the first real house I've ever lived in."

"We finally have space to breathe," my father said. He stopped unpacking and put his hands around my mother's waist, pulling her to him. "This will be a fresh start," he said, and kissed her on her mouth. He let go of her and smiled at my sister and me. "For all of us."

chapter 5

The new house failed to make my mother happy for very long. After a few weeks, I could sense that whatever she'd been looking for hadn't materialized. She seemed disappointed, like a kid who'd asked for a bicycle for her birthday and got socks instead. Even Sarai, who was changing from a baby into a person, rarely made her smile. Everyone upset her, especially me.

In July, my mother enrolled me in a four-week day camp. She told me it would be fun, although I suspected she just wanted me out of the house. Still, I liked the camp. The kids were nice and so were the counselors. We made brightly colored lanyards out of plastic strings, and pot holders decorated with gold-painted macaroni. We played games and went swimming every day. I even got to ride the bus to camp by myself.

For the last day of camp, we had been divided into two teams: yellow and green. Color games, the counselors called it, and sent a note home telling our parents we were supposed to wear a T-shirt with our team color. I was on the yellow team. That morning, after I brushed my teeth, I walked into my room to get dressed. As she did every morning, my mother had laid out my clothes: panties, socks, shorts, and a T-shirt. I picked up the shirt; it was pink, not yellow. Thinking my mother had forgotten about the note, I hollered for her. When she didn't come, I put on everything except the shirt.

such a pretty picture

I found her in the kitchen. Sarai sat at the table in her booster chair; my mother sat sideways on the chair next to her.

My mother held a spoonful of scrambled eggs in front of Sarai. "Have a little."

Sarai shook her head no. "I want noodles." My sister, who fed herself perfectly well, refused to eat anything but macaroni and cheese. The terrible twos, I'd heard my mother tell my grandmother over the phone, although Sarai was almost three.

"I'm supposed to wear a yellow shirt," I said, holding the pink shirt out for my mother to see.

My mother put the spoon down on the table and stood up to face me. "Your yellow shirt is dirty."

"It's color day. My team is yellow, not pink."

"Wear that shirt."

"But my counselor said . . ."

"I don't care what your counselor said. I'm telling you to wear the pink." My mother snatched the shirt out of my hands and pulled me closer to her. Her fingernails dug into my arm.

The intensity of her anger scared me. I worried that she might go blind again.

"Why are you so difficult?" She let go of my arm, pulled the shirt over my head, and then grabbed one arm to try to force it into the sleeve.

"Mommy, you're hurting me. Stop!" I squirmed out of her reach. Tears ran down my face onto the collar of the bunched-up T-shirt. Snot poured out of my nose.

"Stop!" Sarai yelled.

I wasn't sure if she was yelling at my mother or me, or both of us.

"Finish putting the shirt on," my mother snapped at me.

"But it's pink." I wiped the snot with the back of my hand.

Sarai pushed her eggs off the table. Her plastic dish hit the floor with a clatter, and she screamed.

"I'm on the yellow team," I sobbed.

My mother covered her face with her hands. "I can't deal with this."

I knew I should stop whining, but I didn't want to be the only kid in a pink shirt. "I'll wear the dirty yellow one."

"Enough!" My mother took a step toward me.

"But no one will know."

"I said enough." She raised her hand, and I felt the sting of her slap. She'd never slapped me like that before.

"You hit my face," I wailed. I imagined the imprint of her hand on my skin. "Why did you hit me?"

She picked up the plastic dish off the floor. "Go wash your face and put that shirt on the rest of the way." She folded her arms across her chest. "Hurry, so you don't miss the bus."

Ten minutes later, along with my mother and my sister, I waited at the bus stop a few doors down from our house. Sarai, probably exhausted from the fighting, sat half-asleep in her stroller. No longer crying, and dressed in my pink shirt, I stood next to my mother. The shirt was a soft cotton but it felt like wool against my skin.

We were there for only a few minutes when Marty, a seven-year-old and the only other kid who took the bus from that stop, marched up to us. His lemon-colored T-shirt matched his hair exactly. Directly behind us, a teenage boy started a rusted lawn mower. Sarai put her hands over her ears and my mother bent down to soothe her.

"Your shirt is pink!" Marty shouted over the sputtering lawn mower. "You're going to get in big trouble."

"Marty, manners," his mother said, and smiled apologetically at my mother.

My mother scrutinized me as she worried the inside of her mouth, a rose-flush rising in her cheeks. My chest constricted.

"It's my fault." I faced Marty's mother. "I spilled grape juice on my yellow shirt. My mommy tried to wash it but she couldn't get it out in time."

such a pretty picture

"Grape juice is the worst," Marty's mother said. "I'm sure the counselors will understand."

My mother nodded and squatted next to me. "My protector," she whispered in my ear.

Her voice sounded like warm milk and honey. "I love you, Mommy." I melted into her arms.

She held me until the school bus pulled up in front of us. As I climbed on and took my seat next to Marty, I knew I'd face questions for the rest of the day about my pink shirt, but I no longer cared.

chapter 6

The hitting continued. By the end of the summer, any mistake I made, no matter how small, resulted in hard slaps across my face or on my arms. My mother's soft, loving hands, hands I'd always thought could have belonged to Snow White or Sleeping Beauty, had turned bony and brittle. They reminded me of the Wicked Stepmother or some other bad witch. I was afraid of her hands. I was afraid of her.

My father, on the other hand, was hardly home and when he was, he ignored me. In my child's logic, I'd hoped that might be enough. That if my father proved he'd stopped loving me, my mother would forgive us for the bath. With time, I'd understand that she was incapable of blaming him for what happened. Perhaps it was unconscious, but my mother had transferred all of her anger onto five-and-a-half-year-old me. By the time I started kindergarten in September, I couldn't get through breakfast without a slap. Each morning I'd arrive at school with scarlet cheeks and puffy eyes. One time, my teacher asked me if anything was wrong at home. I told her everything was fine. I knew better than to tell the truth. Thankfully, she never asked again.

As leaves on the trees changed from green to orange, my self-hatred grew. A ball of despair formed deep inside of me, and I started to wonder if it would be better if I disappeared. I thought about running away but I figured I'd be found. Duncan, who was eight and lived next door, had tried to run away.

such a pretty picture

His parents found him before dinner. I needed to find another way—I wanted to make my mother happy. Then my friend Sharon's grandmother died.

Sharon lived three houses down from us in a house identical to ours except that it was blue. An only child, she lived with her parents and her grandmother. Sharon's parents were young and Jewish, like my parents. My mother sometimes had coffee with her mother. A few days after her grandmother died, my mother and I went to Sharon's house to pay what my mother said were our respects.

My father had come home early but he didn't want to go. "I hate that shit. Take Andrea, I'll watch Sarai."

"Will Sharon's grandmother be there?" I asked my mother. It was a chilly early November evening. I was wearing my best coat—olive green with a fake leopard collar—a matching hat, and my black velvet Mary Jane shoes. My mother had dressed up too. Wearing her cashmere coat over her good black dress, she carried a casserole dish. It felt like we were going to a party.

"Sharon's grandmother died," my mother said. "She's gone."

"Is she gone forever?" I'd never known anyone who died.

"Yes, Andrea. When people die, they're gone forever."

"Is forever long?"

My mother sighed. "Forever is forever," she said with an edge to her voice.

When we got to Sharon's house, Sharon's mother and two uncles sat on boxes in the center of the living room. "It's called sitting shiva," my mother told me. "It's the way we grieve when our relatives die." Sharon sat on her father's lap. She waved to me but didn't run over like she usually did. The family was dressed in black, even Sharon.

I saw a table against the wall loaded with food—casseroles, brisket, cakes, fancy cookies, knishes, and loaves of challah bread. People crowded into the living room. Except for Sharon and me, they were all adults. Most of them stood in groups talking and snacking on food they'd piled onto small paper plates. My mother had told me that when people grieved they were sad, but the people who were eating didn't seem sad at all. Only Sharon's family acted sad. None of them were eating, and I could tell from the look on their faces how much they missed Sharon's grandmother. They must have loved her a lot.

After that night, I knew I needed to die. I wasn't exactly sure what dying was, but I knew it was forever, and that sounded long enough. If I were gone forever maybe my mother would miss me. Maybe she'd cry for me. And if I got lucky maybe she'd even love me again.

Like my old preschool in Queens, my elementary school in Commack was within walking distance from our house. Each day, my mother and Sarai dropped me off in the morning and picked me up at lunchtime.

A week after Sharon's grandmother died, I ran to my mother and sister waiting for me as usual outside of my school. "I missed you," I said, kissing the top of Sarai's golden head. I told her this every afternoon. I wanted her to know that I loved her and that, although my mother loved her more than me, I wasn't jealous— even though I was. I also wanted my mother to see me being nice to Sarai. I thought if she noticed, she'd think I was good. And maybe, one day, if I was good enough, she'd love me like she did before the bath.

When we got home, the table was set for my lunch. "Sarai and I already ate," my mother said. "I'll make you a sandwich after I put her down." She led Sarai into her bedroom.

After they left, my stomach growled and I didn't want to wait. I went to the refrigerator and grabbed a carton of milk and a bottle of chocolate syrup. I took them back to the table and poured the milk and the syrup into the glass my mother had left out. After stirring the milk exactly like my mother did, I took a sip. It tasted sweet and good. Proud that I'd taken care of myself, I put the syrup and the milk back into the refrigerator.

"What a mess," my mother said when she came into the kitchen a few minutes later. She stood with her hands on her hips, staring at the floor. I followed her gaze. The white linoleum was spotless except for a trail of chocolate syrup leading from the table to the refrigerator.

"I'm sorry." I pushed my milk away.

"You're always sorry," she said, and walked to the sink. "Why can't you be more careful?" Turning on the water, she picked up the big orange sponge she used to clean messes.

"I don't know." I started to cry. I stood up, wanting to run, but my body froze.

"Stop crying." She walked toward me, shaking the sponge in her hand. "You're driving me crazy!" she yelled, and slapped my face. The wet sponge felt like a thousand jellyfish stinging my skin. I started to cry harder. "I told you to stop crying." She hit me again, this time so hard, I almost lost my balance.

"Please don't hit me!" I shouted, and ran to my bedroom. Shutting the door behind me, I threw myself onto my bed and buried my face in my pillow to muffle my sobs. I hated myself for making her so mad. I needed to do something to make her feel better.

I had stopped crying by the time my mother tapped on my door. She cracked it open, but didn't come inside. "I have a headache," she said. "I'm going to lie down. I left you a sandwich and a fresh glass of milk on the table."

I waited until I heard her shut her bedroom door. My mother kept all of my shoes in their boxes neatly stacked on my closet floor. I took off my school shoes, but I didn't put them into their box as I was taught. For once I wasn't worried she'd yell at me when she noticed. I'd be dead by then.

Andrea Leeb

Picking up the empty shoebox, I tiptoed from my room to the bathroom. First, I grabbed a wad of toilet paper, then a handful of cotton balls from the silver jar my mother kept on the counter. I knew there was a pair of tweezers on the second shelf of the medicine cabinet because I'd seen my mother use them to pluck her eyebrows. Trying not to make any noise, I stood on the toilet and reached for them. One by one, I put everything into the shoebox. Then I went into my father's study. He kept a dispenser of Scotch tape on top of his desk. He hated when I played with it.

The tape dispenser made the box heavy. Afraid of dropping it, I held it against my chest with both hands until I made it back to my room.

I started with my ears, pushing the cotton balls deep into the holes. Next, I went to my nose. I stuck a wad of toilet paper into each of my nostrils, shoving it in as far as I could with my fingers. When I couldn't get it in any further, I pushed it with the blunt end of the tweezers. I saved my mouth for last, taping it shut one piece at a time. By the time I finished, I'd used all of the tape. I had plugged any hole where air could get in. Closing my eyes, I held my breath. I was going to die.

I don't remember how long I lay there, but I do recall that my mother cried when she found me. She sat down on my bed and gently peeled the tape off my mouth. It stung, but I was so happy to have her touch me, it was worth it.

I'd pushed the toilet paper so far up my nose, she had to use the tweezers to pull it all out. When she finished, she lay down next to me and held me tight. She hadn't held me like that since the day she got her sight back.

"My poor baby. What have I done to you?"

"I'm sorry, Mommy." Tears started rolling down my cheeks.

"Shush." She put two fingers against my lips. Her hands felt soft and beautiful again—Snow White hands. "I love you, Andrea."

"I love you too, Mommy."

such a pretty picture

"I promise I'll do better."

I wasn't sure if I believed her but I wanted to; I needed to. No matter what happened or what she did to me, she was the person I loved the most. And that afternoon, as I pressed my body against my mother's, I shut my eyes and let her rock me into a gentle afternoon sleep.

chapter 7

A few weeks later, on the Friday before Thanksgiving, the world turned upside down. It was a cool cloudy day. My father had not yet left for work and my mother was walking me to school without my sister. As we walked, my mother held my pink gloved hand in her black leather one. In my mind, I felt our skin touching through our gloves.

I was happy that morning. My mother had kept her promise to do better and had stopped hitting me. Although I did not know it then, she'd never hit me again. In retrospect, it must have been hard for my mother to admit to herself that she was destroying me with her slaps. For me, the impact of her stopping proved to be immense. I took it as evidence of her love, evidence that gave me the hope I needed to survive. Evidence that I carry with me still.

"Mommy is going back to school in January," she told me as we walked.

"To my school?" I took a little skip.

"Not your school, silly," my mother said. "The college where Daddy works."

"Who will take care of us?" I stopped walking. I'd just gotten her back. I didn't want to lose her again.

"It'll only be two days a week. I'm going to ask Nanny to stay with you girls until I get home." She squatted next to me and took my face between her gloved hands. "You're too young to

such a pretty picture

understand, but I have to do something for myself." She gave me a light kiss on my nose and stood up. "Come on," she said, and gave my hand a tug. "If we don't get moving, you'll be late."

That afternoon Nanny and Sarai picked me up. "Is Mommy already in college?" I asked my grandmother as we started walking. Sarai walked between us, holding each of our hands. Like me, Sarai wore gloves—red, not pink—but my grandmother's hands were bare. I wondered if she felt cold.

"Mommy's at the grocery store," Nanny said. "She's getting the Thanksgiving turkey."

I went over the months in my head. "January is after November," I said.

"What's in January?"

"In January, Mommy is going to Daddy's college." We stopped at the curb. A crossing guard held up a stop sign. "She's going back to school." I waited for my grandmother to respond.

At first, she didn't say anything, not until after the crossing guard put the stop sign down and waved us across the street. "Your father has a good job," my grandmother said more to herself than to me. She shook her head. "Whadda she need college for?"

Back at home, my grandmother had just given Sarai and me our lunch when I heard the front door open. Afraid I'd get smacked for tattling about my mother going to college, I pushed my food away.

"Mom," my mother yelled from the hall. She slammed the door behind her. "Have you heard?" she asked, running into the kitchen.

"Dahling." My grandmother got up and walked to my mother. "What's wrong?"

"Ma," my mother sobbed. "Someone shot him."

"Shot who?"

I stopped eating and held my breath. Did someone shoot my father?

"The president . . . Someone shot President Kennedy." My mother collapsed into my grandmother's arms and I let out a sigh of relief.

For the next four days our house filled with people. Both sets of my grandparents, my father's students, and my parents' friends huddled together, crying while they watched the TV. The handsome president with the pretty wife and two little kids was, like Sharon's grandmother, gone. Forever. All of the adults around me acted like they were falling apart, and I started to realize that forever might be more than a long time. I began to understand that the president wasn't coming back. He'd never see his pretty wife or his two little kids again; he'd never be able to tell them he loved them. My parents told me that he was in a good place but it sounded to me like he was all alone. I promised myself that no matter what, I'd never try to die again.

The first week after the president was killed nothing seemed normal. We even skipped Thanksgiving. My mother had been putting her newly purchased groceries into our station wagon when she learned about the assassination. In her haste to get home, she had left the turkey on the roof of the car. Instead of turkey, we ate Chinese food out of cartons.

Chanukah fell two weeks after Thanksgiving. My parents were not religious, but we always celebrated Chanukah. That year was no different and, for eight nights, we lit the menorah and opened presents. My parents tried to act happy, but I could tell they were pretending. They weren't the only ones. All of the grown-ups—my teacher, my grandparents, even the mailman—still seemed sad. They acted as if someone had dropped a gray blanket over them and they didn't know how to crawl out from under it.

I felt a shift a few days before Christmas. Maybe it was the decorations or the music, or maybe everyone just got tired of being

such a pretty picture

sad, but one by one the adults began to smile again. Although half the families on our block were Jewish, our next-door neighbors and the people who lived next to them decided to throw a big Christmas Eve party. Two parties combined into one, they invited the entire block—adults only.

Christmas Eve, the night of the party, my father, my sister, and I sat in the living room watching a Christmas cartoon while we waited for the sitter to come. My sister and I were curled up on each side of my father—she in her footed pajamas, me in a pink nightgown with a ruffled collar. My father looked handsome in his black suit and red silk tie. His glasses had slid down his nose, and I pushed them up with the tip of my finger.

"The sitter is late," my mother said as she walked into the room. She'd bought a new dress for the party. Black velvet and slim-fitted, it had a matching collarless jacket with a single rhinestone button at the neck. She stopped in front of the couch and smiled at us. "My perfect little family," she said. "You all look so cute."

"And you look breathtaking," my father replied.

My mother sat down on a chair catty-corner from the couch. The phone rang immediately. "Not a minute to unwind . . ." She sighed, stood up, and walked to the kitchen where we kept our phone.

A few minutes later, she came back. "The sitter's sick."

"Can you find someone else?" my father asked.

"Not last minute on Christmas Eve. You go. I'll stay home with the girls."

"It's right next door," he said. "We can both go."

"They're too young. What if there's a fire?"

"There won't be a fire," he said. "We'll take turns checking on them."

"I don't know." My mother shook her head.

Andrea Leeb

"We've been looking forward to a night out." My father stood up and grabbed my mother's hand. "They'll be fine. I promise."

My father woke me out of a deep sleep. I didn't know what time it was, or how long my parents had been at the party. My mother had put us both to bed before they went out. She'd left the hall light on and my door open, but my father had shut it.

"Hello, cutie," he whispered. He stood over my bed with a red Santa hat askew on his head. He smelled of alcohol and smoke.

I pulled my blanket up to my chin. "Where's Mommy?" I asked. My father never came into my room without my mother. Seeing him standing there, I felt my dinner rising into the back of my throat.

"Mommy is still at the party." He untangled my fingers from the blanket and pulled the bedcovers back. "Daddy wants to play with you." He lifted my nightgown over my head.

The next morning, I woke dressed in my nightgown again. For a minute, I thought that my father coming into my room had been a nightmare. I climbed out of bed. Squeezing my eyes shut, I pulled back the sheets. *Please let it be a bad dream*, I prayed. But when I opened them, the first thing I saw was the big round stain my father had made when he'd wet the bed. Shuddering, I pulled the blanket over the sheet. Hours later, I'd come back to my room and see that the sheets had been changed. I had been toilet trained for as long as I could remember and had never had an accident. I wondered if my mother would ask about the spot, but she didn't. Not that time, and not any of the times that followed.

Tiptoeing into the hallway, I checked Sarai's room first. Her bed was empty and my parents' bedroom door shut. My mother must have taken her into bed with them during the night. I stood in front of the door and thought about going in, but even thinking

such a pretty picture

about crawling into bed with my father made me itch. I would read in the living room until everyone got up.

I saw the bicycle as soon as I walked into the room. It was pink and white with silver streamers, the most beautiful bike I'd ever seen. Dropping my book, I ran to it and kissed it—twice. My parents had told me I'd have to wait until I turned six to get a bike, so I'd been hoping to get one for my birthday in March. Stroking the bike's smooth metal surface, I tried to figure it out. It was Christmas, but I didn't get Christmas presents. Maybe they were holding the bike for one of our neighbors. A Christmas surprise for some other girl. But it was exactly the bike I wanted. It had to be for me.

"Do you like it?" I heard my father ask. Both my parents and Sarai stood under the archway separating the living room and the hallway.

"It's mine!" Sarai ran to the bicycle.

My father took a few steps and picked her up. "You just got a tricycle for Chanukah. This one is for Andrea."

"Daddy bought it yesterday," my mother said. "He saw it in the store and couldn't resist. We'd agreed to wait for your birthday, but last night he decided he couldn't wait. Your father loves you so much."

"You've been such a good girl." My father winked at me.

Later that morning, he offered to teach me to ride. As I dressed, my mother insisted I put a heavy sweater over my shirt, and my coat on over that. She even made me wear a woolen hat. I could barely move.

"Do you think it's too cold?" she asked my father. I stood at the front door next to my bike, anxious to go and hoping she wouldn't stop us.

My father, dressed in a pair of dungarees, a sweatshirt, and the black high-top sneakers he wore to work around the house, laughed. "It's been in the mid-forties all week."

"Okay, but if she gets cold, bring her right back."

"Your mother has you dressed for the Arctic," my father said once we got outside. "You won't be able to ride with all those layers. We'll leave your coat in the car. But don't tell her."

Early Christmas morning, the only people outside were my father and me. He stood holding my bike as I climbed on top. "Take your time," he said.

I took a deep breath and sat for a couple minutes working up the courage to pedal.

"I've got you."

I put one foot down, then the other. He walked and then ran next to me, holding onto the bike as I rode up and down our block—back and forth, waiting until I was stable before he let go.

"I'm riding!" I yelled as I pedaled faster.

I felt as if I were flying over the blacktop. But no matter how fast I pedaled, my father stayed next to me, never more than a few inches away, always there to catch me if I fell.

chapter 8

On a Sunday in late May, I sat on a black Shetland pony. In front of me, a teenage boy held the pony by a lead. Right behind me, Sarai was riding a brown-and-white spotted pony, but instead of a teenage boy, my father led her pony.

I was wearing a sundress, and the pony's fur tickled my bare calves. It was only the three of us that day. My mother, who had been in college for over a year, was at the library working on a paper. We were planning to pick her up later and all go out for Chinese food. I was trying to relax, but as the pony circled the ring I sat stiffly with my hands gripping the saddle horn so hard that my fingers turned white.

"Ange," Sarai yelled for me.

Keeping one hand on the horn, I turned to look at her. Sarai and I were dressed identically that day in navy dresses with tiny white dots, white anklets, and matching navy Keds. The only difference was our hair. Before we left my mother had braided my dark hair and put Sarai's gold ringlets into a puff at the top of her head.

"Having fun, cutie?" my father called to me.

They looked so happy together. Sarai waved again and I forced a smile and waved back at them.

"Do you girls like riding horses?" my father asked after we finished our ride. We were all holding hands as we walked from the pony rides to the entrance of the petting zoo.

"I love it!" Sarai shouted.

"Would you like to take horseback-riding lessons?" My father stopped walking and bent down to talk to us at eye level.

"On ponies?" I asked.

"On horses," he said.

"Full-sized horses!" Sarai screeched, and jumped up and down. "Yes."

"How about you, Ange?"

I didn't answer him. I was taking ballet lessons and I was afraid they wouldn't let me do both.

"Say yes." Sarai grabbed my hand.

"Can I still take ballet?"

My father smiled and nodded.

"Can I get a velvet cap and high boots like the kind the girl wore in *Black Beauty*?" I asked.

"Jesus Christ, you are Marlene's daughter." My father looked up at the sky. "But yes, you can get the velvet hat and the boots. What do you think, cutie?"

"Ange?" Sarai looked at me.

"Okay," I said, and nodded. "But I want the hat first."

Sarai squealed. "Horses! We are going to ride real horses." She threw her arms around my father's neck.

I hugged him too, although the smell of his aftershave and sweat always made me nauseous.

At the petting zoo we started with the cow. My father held each of our small hands with his big ones. A reddish cow with a white face stood alone in a smelly dirt pen.

"She's named Daisy," a girl with a cowboy hat and red-checked shirt told us.

"Can I pet her?" Sarai asked my father.

"One at a time," my father said, and lifted her up.

When it was my turn, I shook my head no and took a step back.

"Don't be afraid, the cow won't hurt you." My father lifted me up by my waist. "See how sweet she is."

such a pretty picture

I leaned away from him toward the cow. "Her eyelashes are the same color as her fur," I said. Her brown eyes looked leaky, and I wondered if she was crying. I felt sorry for her, locked in that little pen without any grass to chew on or other cows to play with. "Don't be sad, Daisy," I whispered, and reached out to touch her forehead with my fingertips. "Someday someone will come and take you to a nice green pasture."

We went to the sheep pen next. There were three sheep inside, and although it was even smellier than the cow pen, it was filled with hay. All I could think about was how much happier the sheep looked than Daisy. The sheep were shorter, and my father didn't have to lift us to pet them. I stood in front of a white one with a black face and opened my fingers wide so I could feel her wooly coat between my fingers.

"Can we get one as a pet?" Sarai asked my father.

My father laughed. "Our backyard is too small."

"How about a lamb?" she persisted.

"How about I try to talk your mother into letting you each get a hamster?"

"I don't know what a hamster is," Sarai said.

"Well, that's part of the surprise. Right, Ange?" My father winked at me and for once his wink made me laugh.

Before we went into the goat pen, we decided to wash our hands and stop for a snack. My father bought each of us a small red-and-white bag filled with buttered popcorn and led us to a bench in front of the pen.

"You forgot to get a soda," Sarai said. "Mommy always gets us soda."

My father shook his head and sighed. "Sit here until I come back. Don't move and don't talk to any strangers."

"It was a trick," Sarai said to me once my father was out of earshot. "I want to feed the goats."

"No, Daddy said don't move."

"You're such a fraidy-cat."

Before I could stop her, she ran into the pen. The goats were on top of her within seconds. She dropped the popcorn but they surrounded her, nipping at her dress. One of them jumped up and pulled the ribbon out of her hair. She screamed. My father appeared out of nowhere. Pushing past the attendants, he scooped Sarai into his arms. Sobbing, she buried her face into his neck as he wrapped his arms around her and made his way past the milling goats. I ran to them as they came out.

"You're both safe," he said, and scooped me up with his free arm.

A few minutes later he realized his pants had been soiled by the goats. When he noticed, I worried he would spank Sarai for not listening, but he didn't. He never said a word about it. He just brushed himself off and took us to the rest of the pens. Our hero daddy for the entire day.

chapter 9

By the time I started second grade, my father came to my room regularly. He never put his penis inside of me, but he touched me with his fingers and he taught me how to touch him until he came—a sticky spurt on my nightgown, my bed, or my naked skin. When he was done, he would always kiss the top of my head. "Our secret, cutie," he'd say to me with a wink.

As a teenager and a young adult, I would tell myself that because he didn't penetrate me with his penis, the abuse was not that bad. That I had no reason to complain, and at least he'd left me a virgin. It was only later, after I'd gotten help for the damage he had done to me, that I finally understood that penile penetration was a distinction without a difference. Rape is rape.

"Why are we here?" my mother asked Mrs. Powers, my second-grade teacher. My mother and I sat in two small student chairs across from Mrs. Powers, who sat, hands folded in front of her, behind her desk. Mrs. Powers was an older woman. Tall and thin, she had a sharp nose, white hair cut into a pageboy, and the straightest posture I had ever seen. Everything about her looked stern and strict. She wore the same outfit every day: a dark woolen skirt, a starched white shirt buttoned up to her throat, beige stockings, and thick black-soled shoes. My mother said she dressed like a retired nun.

Andrea Leeb

"I'm worried about Andrea," Mrs. Powers said. She had been my teacher only since January, when we'd moved from Commack to Oyster Bay, which was also on Long Island. "Another fresh start," my father had said. I'd hoped it meant he'd stop coming into my room. It didn't.

Our new home was a fancy two-story house with four bedrooms and a den. Years later, I'd ask my mother how they afforded it on a professor's salary. "I never thought about it," she said, shrugging. "Your father was always a bit of a hustler."

"Worried?" My mother shifted in the tiny chair. "She gets all As."

"She cries. Sometimes several times a day. It interrupts the class. I have to put her in the hallway until she stops."

My mother looked at me. I thought she was about to say something but instead she stood up. She smoothed the creases out of her pink silk shift and stared at Mrs. Powers. "Before we continue, could you please get me an adult chair?"

Mrs. Powers leaned over her desk. "Parents always sit on student chairs. Even fathers."

My mother had her back to me, so I couldn't see her face. I wondered if she was scared. Everyone at school, including the principal, was afraid of Mrs. Powers.

"I'm sure you can find a chair in one of the empty classrooms." She paused. "Or we can reschedule this conference for another date once an appropriate chair is located."

"I don't know why you're being so difficult." Mrs. Powers sighed and stood up. "But I'll be right back."

"We'll be here," my mother said. She waited until Mrs. Powers shut the door behind her before she spoke to me. "Is she telling the truth? Are you really crying during the school day?" She sounded angry.

"Sometimes," I mumbled, and put a strand of hair into my mouth.

such a pretty picture

"Don't chew your hair." My mother pulled the hair out of my mouth. "It's not good to cry in public. People don't like little girls who cry."

We didn't say another word until Mrs. Powers returned, dragging a large chair with two wooden arms.

"Andrea, can you explain to us why you cry?" Mrs. Powers asked, once she'd taken her place behind her desk.

"I . . . I don't know." My eyes filled with tears. Afraid they'd both be angry with me, I stared at the floor.

"You don't know why you cry?" Mrs. Powers asked.

"No," I said, my eyes still on the floor.

"Is everything all right at home?"

"Everything is fine," my mother answered. She sat posture-perfect, her eyes locked on Mrs. Powers. "Why would you ask Andrea that question?"

"The crying, the hair chewing, and look at her nails. She's bitten them down to the quick. The child is picking herself to death. Something is obviously wrong."

"She's sensitive." My mother crossed her arms. "To be honest, I think she's afraid of you."

"It has nothing to do with me," Mrs. Powers said. "I haven't said anything to Andrea, but she's been telling lies in class."

I twisted the end of my hair, fighting the urge to put it in my mouth. What did Mrs. Powers think I lied about? I couldn't remember ever lying to her. I thought about my father, about the deals we made and how we lied to my mother. How had Mrs. Powers figured it out? I'd never told anyone.

"What did you lie about?" my mother asked me.

"I don't know." I wished I could run out of the classroom.

"During show-and-tell last week, she told the class that she was on a train with a bomb. Quite the story. Told, I am sure, to get attention."

Andrea Leeb

My mother uncrossed her arms and gave Mrs. Powers a pink-frosted smile. Her lipstick matched her dress and her shoes. "Is that why you made me come in? I had to get a babysitter for my other daughter so you could tell me this?" My mother shook her head. "She wasn't lying. We took the girls to Washington, to an antiwar demonstration. There was a bomb threat on the train. They evacuated us for over an hour, although in the end there wasn't an actual bomb."

"I read about that demonstration," Mrs. Powers said. She tapped her fingers against her desk. "The newspaper said it was hippies and radicals. Troublemakers."

"A peaceful protest," my mother said. "We're worried about Vietnam. We thought it important that we go and take the girls. We don't want our daughters growing up in a bubble."

"I see." Mrs. Powers pursed her lips. I could tell that she was annoyed with my mother, but at least they weren't talking about me.

"And I see that you don't approve of our politics." My mother stood up. "I think we are done here. I'm not sure how this is any of your business."

"Mrs. Leeb, I'm sorry we got off track, but I didn't ask you to come in to talk about your politics." Mrs. Powers folded her hands in front of her. "I asked you to come in because your child is falling apart, and you need to do something about it."

"I think I've heard enough," my mother said. "Andrea, get your things together."

My schoolbooks and my lunch box with a picture of the Beatles on the front were piled on the floor next to my chair. I picked them up and followed my mother. She opened the door, but before we walked out, she turned to Mrs. Powers.

"My daughters are both enrolled in horseback riding and dance classes, and as you are well aware, Andrea is reading three grade levels ahead. I can assure you she is not falling apart."

such a pretty picture

We left the classroom and walked into the empty hallway. The janitors must have recently finished mopping, because the floors were wet and the air smelled of ammonia.

"I don't know who that old witch thinks she is," my mother said as we made our way out of the school and into the parking lot.

We drove home without talking. I knew my mother was mad, but I couldn't tell if she was angry with me or Mrs. Powers, or both of us. My best bet was to stay quiet and hope she'd forget about it.

"I need to talk to you before we go in," my mother said when we pulled into the driveway.

My lunch box on my lap, I traced my fingers over John, Paul, George, and Ringo's smiling faces.

"Look at me," my mother said. She waited until I met her eyes before speaking again. "The crying has to stop."

"I'm sorry." I bit my lip hard.

"You're giving your teacher a bad impression. She thinks there's something wrong with you." She reached over and stroked my cheek.

Her fingertips felt like velvet. How could I tell her that Mrs. Powers was right? If I did, I might lose her forever.

"I won't cry in front of her anymore," I said, although I wasn't sure I could stop. "I promise."

"That's my good girl." She kissed me with her frosted lips.

My father taught night classes twice a week. On those nights, my mother always waited up to serve him dinner. That night was one of my father's teaching nights. After my mother came in and kissed me goodnight, I pulled out a little flashlight I'd won as a prize in summer camp and a book. I wanted to make sure I stayed awake until my father came home. I knew my mother would tell him about Mrs. Powers, and I needed to know how he'd respond. He might think I'd broken my promise not to tell and I was afraid of what he might do to me. Although I knew there was nothing I could do to change his reaction, I wanted to be ready.

When I heard the front door open and close, I waited until I thought it was safe. I tiptoed down the stairs, careful not to make any noise, and stood flat against the wall next to the archway leading into our kitchen. If they caught me, I could pretend to be thirsty.

"Mrs. Powers told me that Andrea cries every day," my mother said. She must have assumed Sarai and I were both sound asleep, because she didn't even bother whispering. I heard every word.

"Andrea's hypersensitive," my father said.

"She said Andrea is falling apart. She made it sound like she's a mess. Like she's mentally ill."

"She could have a point," my father said.

"Why would you say that?"

"Andrea has problems," he said. "We give her everything, but she's never happy." A beat later, "Marlene, could you make me another drink?"

"You've had two already." But my mother must have gotten up to make him one, because a minute or so later I heard the sound of the refrigerator door open and the clink of ice cubes against glass.

"Look, I know this is upsetting," my father said, "but we may have to face it. Andrea might be emotionally disturbed."

"Do you think we should get her help?" my mother asked. "Send her to a child psychiatrist?"

"No," my father said loudly. "I mean, not yet."

"Why would we wait?"

"Right now, she's a crazy little girl. Hysterical. If we make too big a deal, you never know what she'll say to get attention." My father paused. "Besides, kids usually outgrow these things."

such a pretty picture

My parents grew silent for a minute. I pictured my mother thinking about what my father had just said. *Did she think I was crazy too?* I squeezed my eyes shut so I wouldn't start to cry.

"That teacher is so nosy," she said.

"Don't worry, she isn't going to do anything. And if Andrea doesn't get better, we can always send her away to get help. There are hospitals for kids with serious problems."

Back in my room, I climbed into bed and got under the covers. I knew my father had had at least three drinks, so I prayed he'd pass out drunk until morning, that he wouldn't come to my room. When my father drank, it could go either way. I closed my eyes but was too scared to sleep, my head filled with chatter. I went over and over the things Mrs. Powers and my parents had said about me. I didn't understand everything, but I understood enough to be worried about what they might do to me or where they might send me. They all scared me, but especially my father. I needed to stop crying and convince myself that everything was fine.

chapter 10

My mother's words stayed with me: "People don't like little girls who cry." I did my best not to cry in school or anytime where anyone could see me, and I tried to keep any interaction with Mrs. Powers to a minimum. I was furious with her and wished she had minded her own business, but my father was right not to worry about her. She never called my mother again and for the most part, she ignored me, although there were times when I caught her studying me as if she were trying to figure something out. For years afterward, I would think about her as the meanest teacher I ever had. I was thirty-three before I realized she was the only teacher and one of the few adults in my life to see that I was suffering. Unfortunately, despite her name, she was powerless to give me the help I needed.

The following summer, my family settled into its version of normal. My father went to work, my mother continued going to school, and they both became more politically active. For years, my parents had been involved with what my mother told me was civil rights. They'd gone to marches, including the big march in Washington where Martin Luther King Jr. spoke.

Since taking us to the antiwar demonstration in April, they'd been more vocal about Vietnam. But beginning that summer, my parents changed from participants to organizers. On weekends, our living room filled with strangers planning marches or sit-ins.

such a pretty picture

    My mother usually ran those meetings. As an adult, I'd question the hypocrisy of my mother's commitment to peace and civil rights, given the way my parents treated their own children, but at the time, I felt proud of her. I'd watch from the couch as my normally reserved mother stood in the middle of the group speaking. I could tell that everyone, including my father, admired her. Leading those meetings, my mother looked happy in a way that she never looked when it was only the four of us.

    My father still came to my room at night; not every night, but at least once a week. I did my best to ignore it—to think about something else when he touched me and to forget about it right after. I loved both of my parents unconditionally. I wanted them to love me too. I'd do anything to make sure they did. Even if it meant doing things with my father that I didn't want to do.

Third grade started better than second grade. Pretty and blonde, my teacher was the opposite of Mrs. Powers. Instead of a white pageboy and stern clothing, she wore her hair in a shoulder-length flip, and dressed in brightly colored shifts decorated with geometric designs. I made sure to act like everyone else: a normal kid, not popular but not unpopular either; a nice little girl who got good grades and didn't make any trouble. Invisible.

    That year, Sarai began afternoon kindergarten. My mother—or, on the days my mother had classes, my grandmother—walked her to school. But I had to walk her home. This was not an easy job. Every day as soon as the bell rang, I'd run full speed to her classroom. The only time I was ever late she left without me and snuck onto a school bus. Luckily the driver realized she wasn't one of his regular riders before he took off, but for a few horrible minutes I was terrified I'd lost her.

    One day in late March, I made my way to her classroom like I always did. I got there just as her teacher opened the door. Dressed in a red plaid jumper with a matching headband holding back her honey-colored curls, Sarai looked angelic. The only clue of her true impish nature were her knees, which were scraped and bruised from jumping and falling.

"Hold my hand," I instructed as we walked into the packed hallway.

"I'm big enough to walk by myself." Sarai stomped a Mary Jane–clad foot. A group of fifth graders pushed their way past us, almost knocking her over.

"I'm responsible for you." I grabbed her hand. "Mommy will kill me if anything happens to you," I said, and steered her through the maze of screaming children.

"Look it's Mommy," Sarai said as we walked onto the sidewalk. My mother stood alone, just past the throng of children.

I hadn't expected her. She picked us up only on the days it snowed or rained, and that afternoon it felt like spring—the kind of sunny day where you could keep your coat open or take it off altogether. But my mother had dressed for winter in a heavy black coat that tied at the waist with a belt. As she stood in the warm sunlight, she pulled the belt tighter.

"Mommy!" Sarai ran to her.

"My beautiful girls." Our mother squatted next to her. She pushed her oversized black sunglasses on top of her head. Her eyes were red, the tip of her nose puffy.

I studied her, trying to figure out what was wrong.

"Andrea, come close." She opened her arms, and as I stepped inside of them, she hugged us tightly. "I love you girls to pieces."

Holding hands, the three of us walked to our station wagon. My mother had parked in the back of the lot. We passed lots of open spaces. It seemed strange that she had parked so far away.

such a pretty picture

"Dibs on the front," Sarai said when we got to the car. She put her hand on her hips, challenging me to argue.

For once, I didn't. Peering inside the station wagon, I understood why my mother had parked so far away. Two big suitcases, most of our toys, and a box containing my books were piled into the back. I wondered if we were moving again. We'd been in Oyster Bay for only a little over a year.

"Thank you," my mother mouthed.

I slid behind the front passenger seat. Hearing a squeaking noise, I looked down. Our pet hamsters, Hammy and Hamlet, were in their cage on the floor behind the driver's side.

Sarai turned to face me. "Na-nanna-na, I am in the front," she sang. Then she must have heard the squeaking too. Her eyes fell on the hamster cage.

"Hammy and Hamlet! Can I take them out?"

"The hamsters stay in their cage," my mother said.

"What if we switch, and I only take one out at a time?"

"Everyone stays put including the hamsters. Now turn around and sit down."

I sat quietly while we passed the street leading to our house, and then the intersection into the town of Oyster Bay. When we merged onto the entrance of the Long Island Expressway, I couldn't stand it any longer.

"Where are we going?"

"Nanny's," my mother said. My grandmother lived in the Bronx, about forty-five minutes away.

"Why are we going to Nanny's?"

My mother didn't answer, so I tried a different question.

"Is Nanny okay with us bringing Hammy and Hamlet?" The hamsters terrified my grandmother. She called them rats, and couldn't believe we kept them as pets.

"She's fine with it." My mother sighed. "You're going to be staying with her for a while. She wants you both to be happy."

I sat back against my seat and watched the hamsters. Their cage had two wheels, and they spent all day running around and around in circles. I wondered if they even noticed that they were on the floor of the station wagon instead of their usual spot on the little table in our hallway.

"Is Daddy coming?" Sarai asked.

I'd been wondering the same thing. My father always took charge of packing the car when we went on trips or moved houses.

"No."

I leaned over the seat. "What about you?"

"Not tonight. Not for a little while."

"How long is a little while?" I asked, trying to keep my voice from cracking.

"Enough. Stop acting like Nancy Drew!" Then, more quietly, "We'll talk about it when we get to Nanny's."

"Are you giving us to Nanny?" Sarai asked and began to cry.

I sat on the edge of my seat; my leg began to jiggle. Again, I had the same question. My father constantly threatened to give one or both of us away. I'd always thought he was bluffing, but with him anything was possible.

"Of course not," my mother said.

I sank back into my seat.

"Promise," Sarai said, still crying.

"Pinky promise." My mother took her right hand off the wheel and extended her pinky to my sister. "I love you girls with all my heart."

"I love you too." Sarai wrapped her pinky around my mother's.

"Now, Mommy has to concentrate on driving. Let's all be quiet until we get to Nanny's."

My grandmother's apartment was in a redbrick building on a wide, quiet street lined with trees. Except for the occasional siren

such a pretty picture

in the distance or the sound of a honking horn, you almost forgot you were in a city. My grandmother's two sisters and their families all lived in the building. The idea of so many relatives in one place had always sounded fun to me, but my mother told me she hated all the ruckus when she was growing up. "No privacy; everyone had keys to everyone's apartment. And not one of them could keep a secret if their life depended on it."

When we arrived, there were no parking spaces on the block. "Shit," my mother mumbled as she pulled up next to a car parked in front of my grandmother's building. "Andrea, be a good girl and take Sarai and the hamsters upstairs. Tell Nanny I'm double-parked."

Nanny answered her door after one knock, wearing her usual cotton housedress with silver snaps. My great-aunts and almost every other woman in the building wore identical dresses. The "Yenta uniform," my mother called it. As my grandmother opened the door, I put the hamster cage on the floor and stepped in front of it. I figured the less she saw of them, the better.

"*Mamalehs.*" She kissed and squeezed my face between her hands and then did the same to Sarai.

"Mommy's double-parked," I said after my grandmother stopped kissing us.

"I'd better get down there. I left you a snack in the living room. Go watch TV." Her eyes fell on the spinning hamsters. "And don't let those rodents out of their cage!"

My grandmother's apartment always smelled liked boiled chicken and overcooked brisket. Her living room had just enough space for a couch, two chairs, a coffee table, and a boxy TV. The chairs and couch were all covered in plastic. "It keeps the fabric nice," my grandmother had explained when I asked. The TV sat in the center of the room. My parents had bought it for her earlier that year, the first color one in our family. When they gave it to her, she'd made a tsking sound. "Whadda I need with such a fancy TV?" But she had it on whenever we visited.

Andrea Leeb

I sat down on the plastic couch and put the hamster cage in front of me. As always, the TV was turned to a soap opera. "My programs," my grandmother called them. Sarai switched channels several times, but all she could find were other soap operas and a game show.

"We missed the cartoons," she complained.

"Have some cookies," I said, trying to distract her. I pointed to the plate of cookies and two glasses of milk my grandmother had left for us. The cookies were the good kind from the Snowflake Bakery. My grandmother got them for special occasions only, one more clue that something was wrong.

We ate our cookies without talking. I wasn't hungry, but the cookies were too good to resist.

"Can I take the hamsters out?" Sarai slid to the floor and opened the cage.

"You heard Nanny."

"They need air." She took a hamster in each hand.

"They have air in the cage, silly," I said as she handed me Hamlet, the smaller hamster. I put him on my lap. My skirt had inched up over my knees, and his tiny claws dug into my thighs. "We need to hold them so they don't get loose."

Sarai brought Hammy up to her face. "I love you, Hammy." She had taken off her headband and her curls fell loosely to her shoulders. She kissed the hamster again and smiled. She had recently lost one of her front teeth. She looked so young and innocent; it made me want to cry. "Ange, do you believe her?"

"Believe who?" I needed a second to come up with something to tell her.

"Mommy. Do you think she's giving us to Nanny?" She began to cry.

"Mommy would never give us away, not even to Nanny." I put Hamlet back into his cage and knelt down in front of her. "Don't cry." I wiped her tears away with my fingers. "Everything will be okay."

such a pretty picture

✺ ✺ ✺

"Where are they going to sleep?" my mother asked my grandmother after they brought up the last load. The four of us stood in my grandmother's foyer, surrounded by suitcases, clothing, and toys.

My grandmother's apartment had only two bedrooms, and Uncle Matt, my mother's younger brother, used one of them. When Sarai and I visited, we slept together in the living room on the foldout couch. At age six, Sarai still wet her bed, especially when she got nervous. I couldn't imagine the two of us sleeping on the couch together if we were going to be there for longer than a weekend.

"The little one can sleep in George's bed," my grandmother said, referring to my grandfather, who had died two years before. Like the people on TV, my grandparents had always had twin beds. "I already set up a cot in the dining room for Andrea."

"Mommy's old room," I said. My mother had told me that when she was in high school, her parents had converted the dining room into her bedroom. "I loved that room," she'd said. "The first time I had any privacy." Between the table and the chairs, the room had barely enough space for a cot. But it had been my mother's and it beat sleeping on a lumpy couch drenched in my sister's pee.

"I want Mommy's old room." Sarai stomped her feet.

"You get to sleep in Nanny's room, on a real bed." My mother wiped a drop of sweat off her forehead. "You get the better room." She bent down and kissed the top of Sarai's head.

"That's because you love me most," Sarai said to my mother, and stuck her tongue out at me.

"Your Mommy loves you both the same," my grandmother said.

I put my hair in my mouth to stop myself from correcting her. My mother did love Sarai more, but that was my fault, not my mother's. There were things about our family that no one, not even my grandmother, could ever be told.

My mother checked her watch. "We need to get everything unpacked. I don't want to drive too late."

"Where are you going to sleep?" I asked. "When you come back here?" I knew I shouldn't push her but I couldn't help it.

"Can you sleep with me?" Sarai put her arms around my mother's waist. "Please."

My mother shot me a look. I tensed my shoulders and braced myself: an old reflex. My mother didn't hit me anymore, but sometimes her words stung more than a slap.

"Goddammit, look what you've done to your sister," she said, raising her voice and stroking Sarai's head at the same time.

"Mommy will sleep on the foldout couch when she comes to visit," my grandmother said, patting my mother's arm.

"Why do you have to leave tonight?" Sarai asked, her voice quivering.

My mother frowned at me. "Sometimes I can't figure out if you're selfish or just stupid."

I flinched again. "I'm sorry," I said.

"You're always sorry." My mother untangled herself from Sarai's arms. "Come on, sweetie, let's put your things away." She grabbed a suitcase with one hand and my sister's hand with the other.

There were still so many times my mother made me wish I could disappear. I pressed my fingertips against my eyelids to stop myself from crying but tears flooded down my face anyway.

"*Mamaleh*, don't cry. Mommy's nervous. It has nothing to do with you." My grandmother reached into her housedress and pulled out a butterscotch, her answer to everything. "A little sugar will make you feel better."

I unwrapped the candy and put it in my mouth. Wiping the tears off my face, I sucked on the butterscotch.

such a pretty picture

"See, isn't that better?" She took one of my hands. "Let's go set up your room. When your mother called me this morning to tell me you were coming, I took all the good china out of the credenza so you'd have a special place for your books and your dolls."

"I wanted to apologize before I left." I heard my mother's voice as she entered the room.

It had been a couple of hours since she'd called me selfish and stupid. I sat on the floor with my back to the door, putting my shirts and pants in the bottom shelves of the credenza. I stopped folding, but didn't turn around.

"I'm sorry I was so mean to you." She sat down next to me. "Will you forgive me?"

Nodding yes, I put my head on her shoulder.

Together, we unpacked the rest of my things. When we finished, Sarai and I walked my mother to the elevator. A lingering odor of cigar smoke filled the empty hallway. I stole glances at my mother while we walked. Her clothes were wrinkled and she looked fragile, like Beth in *Little Women*, the sister who died. I thought about the time my mother went blind. Was this change my fault too? Would my mother go blind again, or would something worse happen?

"I want to press." Sarai reached for the button.

The elevator didn't open right away, and I prayed for it to come slowly. I moved my feet into a ballet position, one foot turned out against the arch of the other. When it arrived, I squeezed my mother's hand. Afraid I'd never see her again, I didn't want to let her go.

"I'll be back on Saturday. It's only two days," she said, prying her hands free.

She stepped inside and put one foot in the door to stop it from closing, something she'd told us never to do. *Please change your mind*, I thought. *Step outside and stay.* The elevator buzzed and then buzzed again.

"I have to go." My mother pulled her foot away. "I love you," she said as the door closed.

Sarai and I stood hand in hand, staring at the black door. I expected her to start crying, but she didn't. Neither did I. We were both too drained to cry.

"Do you think she'll be back?" Sarai asked, her eyes still on the elevator door.

"She promised," I said. "Mommy keeps her promises." I hoped it wasn't a lie.

Sarai let go of my hand. "You're right," she nodded. "She'll be back. She'd never leave us."

I faked a smile. "I bet I can beat you back to the apartment." I began to run, not full speed, but fast enough to make it look real as I let her race past me.

That night, after Nanny and Sarai went to bed, I lay on my cot. Although not as lumpy as the foldout couch, it felt hard and unfamiliar. Unable to sleep, I flipped on the light. Earlier, my grandmother had covered the dining room table with an old blanket and instructed me to put the hamster cage on top of it. For once they weren't spinning, and instead curled together in the corner of the cage. I hoped the light wouldn't wake them. My books were lined up on the credenza. Reading seemed better than thinking, so I pulled out *Eight Cousins*. I had read it twice before, but I liked to reread books. I found it comforting to know what was going to happen to the characters, even if they were going to die or have their hearts broken. I could not change the outcome, but it made me feel better to be prepared for any disaster before it happened.

I don't know how long I'd been reading when my uncle came home. Hearing the click of the front door locks opening, I got out of bed and shut off the light. A sliding wooden door separated the dining room and the foyer. It wasn't flush with the wall, and I put my ear against the gap. One, two, three, the locks snapped shut, followed by the rattle of the door chain. I held my breath and waited. My uncle was twenty-two; when we visited, he was usually busy with school or work. I hadn't spent a lot of time with him, but he had always been nice to me. I knew I shouldn't be afraid, but I was all alone in a dark room I'd never slept in before. *Would my uncle be like my father? Would he hurt me with his fingers or make me touch him?* Thinking about it, my legs wobbled underneath me. I leaned against the wall to keep my balance.

The wooden floor groaned as he walked past my room. I didn't move until I heard the toilet flush and the sound of his bedroom door shutting. I waited a little longer. Sliding the door open, I tiptoed into the dark hallway. Somewhere, nearby, a siren wailed. As the sound receded into the city, I took a deep breath and let my body relax.

chapter 11

As promised, my mother came back that weekend. After much begging, she told me that my father had lost his job, and they'd had to sell the house quickly. "I don't want you girls to see people traipsing through your home." Her explanation didn't make sense. When my parents sold their first house, my sister and I didn't have to move out, but I knew not to press it.

We were at Nanny's for two weeks before my mother sent the paperwork needed for us to enroll in our new school. I'd expected her to take us on our first day, but the night before she called Nanny to tell her something had come up.

"I hate her," I said when my grandmother told me. I ran into my room and threw myself onto the cot.

Nanny followed me. "Move over." She sat next to me, squishing me into the wall.

"My mother should be taking us," I said, my voice shaking. My mother knew I hated changing schools. And when Sarai started kindergarten, she had cried every day for the first three months.

"I know it's hard but try to be kind." Nanny stroked my hair. "Your mother would be here if she could."

I nodded to keep my grandmother happy, but I didn't believe her. We needed our mother. Nothing should have been more important than that.

such a pretty picture

The next morning, Nanny took us to P.S. 76, our new school. My mother, my uncle, my aunt, and all my mother's first cousins had attended elementary school there too. This history should have been exciting for us, but it wasn't. We were too scared.

"Do I have to go?" Sarai asked as we entered the school. The three of us held hands. Sarai, who was in the middle, deliberately dragged her feet while we walked.

"Yes, *mamaleh*, but for you it's only a half day." My grandmother pulled Sarai forward.

From day one, Sarai hated that school. She stayed home more than she went. At first, I worried. I didn't want her to get in trouble or get left back. But when I talked to my mother she shrugged. "We'll figure it out once we are settled."

I neither liked nor disliked P.S. 76. I tolerated it. My teacher, Mrs. Schwartz, had white-blue hair and appeared to be even older than Mrs. Powers. On my first day, she made it clear that she did not want a new student assigned to her classroom so late in the year. "Such a burden," I overheard her say to the principal. "What kind of parent changes schools in April?"

During the three months I went to P.S. 76, I didn't make any friends, but I didn't try to either. Like a ghost, I floated in and out of the classroom. I went home every day for lunch, came back on time, did my homework, and didn't talk in class. Once she realized I wasn't going to cause her any trouble, Mrs. Schwartz ignored me.

My mother came to see us every Saturday morning, but my father's whereabouts remained a mystery. My mother and my grandmother both told me he was okay, but when I pressed further, they'd shake their heads and change the subject. Although I was supposed to miss him, a part of me felt glad he was gone. Glad and guilty. I worried constantly that I had caused him to leave, or that my mother had found out about us and she had forced him to go.

The dining room was directly across from the living room and down the hall from the kitchen. Because the door didn't shut all the way, I eavesdropped on adults when they thought I was asleep. My grandmother and my great-aunts made it hard because they spoke to each other in Yiddish. But when my mother visited, everyone switched to English. If I stood still, I heard every conversation in the living room or the kitchen. Each weekend, I listened carefully, hoping I'd learn something about my missing father.

But for weeks, no one said a word.

One Friday night, about six or seven weeks after we moved in, I was up late reading when I heard the keys rattle in the lock. Shutting off my flashlight, I pretended to be asleep. At first, I thought it was my uncle, but then I heard the click of high heels in the hallway, followed by the swishing sound of my grandmother's slippers. *Mommy's here*, I thought, although it made no sense. My mother didn't like to drive at night. She always came on Saturday mornings. *Why was she here?*

"Dahling," I heard my grandmother say. "They're both asleep."

"I'll see them in the morning. If I wake them now, they'll be up all night."

I slid off my cot and tiptoed to my listening place.

"I'll help you with the couch," my grandmother said.

I heard the foldout sofa creak, followed by a small thud as the frame hit the floor.

"Careful," my mother said in a voice barely above a whisper.

"When did he get back?" Nanny never whispered. I didn't think she knew how.

"Tuesday."

"Whadda he got to say for himself?"

"He did it for us. For me and the girls." My mother had stopped whispering, making it easier to hear.

such a pretty picture

"He forged his PhD for you? Don't be a fool."

I put a lock of hair in my mouth, careful to suck on it quietly. I didn't know the word *forge*. I wished I had my father's big Webster dictionary so I could look it up, but my mother hadn't brought it from the Oyster Bay house and my grandmother didn't have one.

"You shoulda left him," my grandmother said after a few seconds.

"The lawyer said that having me there made a big difference with the district attorney."

I took a deep breath. *Please, don't let it be my fault*, I prayed.

"He needed you there so bad, the second he talked his way out of it, he ran off with a blonde *shiksa*."

I knew the Yiddish word *shiksa*. Had my father run off with a Christian woman? If it were true, I felt bad for my mother, but it would mean that my father's disappearance had nothing to do with me. Thinking about that I exhaled and let my body go slack.

"She sent him this."

For a few seconds, I heard nothing. Then faint music.

"A music box?"

"'Lara's Theme' from *Dr. Zhivago*," my mother said. "You know, Omar Sharif and Julie Christy." She went on. "It came in the mail. When he got home and opened the package, he had the nerve to ask me if I wanted it. I thought I might kill him if I didn't get out of the house."

"What a son of a bitch!"

"Shush, you'll wake them."

"Marlene, you are a beautiful woman. You can get married again."

"I have two little girls. No education. And they love their father. He loves them."

"True," my grandmother said. "Whatever you can say about David, he's a good father. He gives those girls everything they could ever want."

Andrea Leeb

Hearing the words *good father* my stomach churned. I swallowed the acid rising in my throat. Everyone thought my father was a good father. Was it true? My mother always told me everything we had—our house, our clothes, and all our toys—were gifts from our father. "He works hard to make us all happy." And there were times, like with the petting zoo, the riding and ballet lessons, or the hamsters, I thought he might actually love us. But other times, especially in the last few months, he acted like he couldn't stand us. Those times, almost everything we did—laughing too loud, or playing in the living room while he watched TV or listened to music—caused him to scream at us, to hit us with the buckle of his belt, or shake us so hard that our heads felt like they might fly off our bodies. Of course, he never did anything like that in front of my grandmother or anyone else except my mother. It was one more family secret.

"Yes," my mother said, "the girls are lucky to have him."

"So, what's next?"

"I'm throwing the box away."

"Not the music box. With David."

"He's home. Working for our friend Harvey, the one who builds houses. He's talking to some colleges about jobs."

"Another college will hire him?"

"You know David, he can spin anything."

"Sweetheart, think about it. You can find someone else."

"I don't want anyone else, Ma. I love him." My mother's voice cracked. "He's my whole life."

Hearing her say that, I thought about the way my father touched me and how I touched him back. "You have to keep this a secret," he said to me over and over again. "Your mother will never forgive us." I had believed him. But at that moment, as I listened to her, I understood for the first time, that what he said wasn't exactly true. My father, the good father, the man who got out of everything, would be forgiven. It was me, and only me, my mother would blame.

chapter 12

I sat cross-legged on the stoop of our building, reading. I'd recently moved from rereading the Alcott books to reading biographies. I preferred books about famous women like Clara Barton, Florence Nightingale, or Betsy Ross, but I wasn't fussy and read pretty much anything I could get my hands on.

It was a Saturday in late July and, like most summer Saturdays, the sidewalk in front of my grandmother's building had turned into a communal living room. It seemed like everyone was outside. The women sat on beach chairs on one side of the building, and the men sat on the other. As usual, the women were dressed in their Yenta uniforms: pastel housedresses, slippers, and nylon stockings rolled down around their ankles. They gossiped in Yiddish, dabbing the sweat off their faces with tissues or handkerchiefs. The men wore short-sleeved shirts and Bermuda shorts with black dress socks and heavy black or brown shoes. They stretched their pale white legs out in front of them and puffed on cigars while they read the *New York Post* or listened to a Yankees game on their transistor radios.

Most of the people who lived on my grandmother's block were old. My mother told me that when she was growing up there had been lots of families, but by 1967 everything had changed. There were only a handful of young families left. Luckily for Sarai, another six-year-old girl, Faye, lived on the third floor of our building. According to my grandmother, Sarai and

Faye were peas in a pod. *Meshugana*, she called them, using the Yiddish word for "crazy people." My books kept me from being lonely, and even if there had been other kids my age around, I still would have spent most of my time reading. I preferred reading about someone else's life to living my own. That Saturday while I read, Sarai and Faye played horses. They'd looped a jump rope around one girl's waist, while the other held onto the handles as if they were reins. Taking turns, they galloped up and down the sidewalk, ignoring the admonishments in Yiddish from the old women on the chairs.

My parents showed up a little after three. Sarai saw them first. "Mommy and Daddy!" She ran to my parents.

Startled, I looked up from my book. My grandmother had told me that my mother would be coming on Sunday that week. I was surprised to see her, but the big shock was seeing my father. He hadn't visited us in the almost four months we'd been living with my grandmother.

My father picked up Sarai and swung her in the air. Her laughter filled the block. My mother saw me and waved me over.

"Andrea." She hugged me. Her perfume smelled unfamiliar: still sweet, but softer and spicier than her old one. Later, she'd tell me she'd decided to try a new scent called Fiji. A perfume she'd wear for the next fifty years. "Hi, cutie." My father gave me a wink. "A hug for Daddy?" Still holding my sister, he bent down. Wincing, I stood on tiptoes and gave his cheek a quick peck.

"I'm Queen of the World," Sarai said. She had moved from my father's arms to his shoulders. There were times Sarai was afraid of my father, but she was still young enough to miss him. In the time I lived with my grandmother, I realized that although I loved him, I felt lighter when he wasn't around. He was easier to love from a distance.

"I kept it a secret. I wanted to surprise them." My grandmother joined us and kissed my mother's cheek.

such a pretty picture

"I know how they love surprises." My mother smiled. "And we have another one. A big one."

"Are we getting presents?" Sarai clapped her hands.

"Better than presents." My mother laughed. "We are moving to Florida."

"Us too?" I asked, a little afraid of the answer.

"All four of us," she said.

"When?" I asked.

"We're leaving tomorrow," my father said. "It will be a fresh start."

That night after dinner, my parents told us more about the move. We sat in the living room, my mother and grandmother on the couch, my father across from them on one of the plastic-covered chairs. For once, Nanny allowed Sarai to take the hamsters out, and the two of us sprawled on the floor petting them.

My father had gotten a new job teaching at a community college in Central Florida. We would be moving to a town called Winter Park.

"You girls will love it," my mother told us. "It's like summer all year round."

"What about Hammy and Hamlet?" Sarai asked. "Are they coming too?"

My father smiled. "Hammy and Hamlet are part of our family."

Early the next morning, Nanny, Sarai, and I stood on the sidewalk watching my parents pack the car. My mother told us the hamsters could sit between Sarai and me but they had to stay in their cage. "If you take them out," my mother said to Sarai, "they ride in the back with the suitcases."

When it was time for us to leave, Sarai and I hugged Nanny.

"My *shaina maidels*." She pulled us against her soft body. "I don't want to let go of you."

"I love you, Nanny," we cried in unison. My grandmother held us closer.

"Don't cry, *mamalehs*, I'll be visiting you soon."

Still crying, we climbed into the back seat. Together, we watched my grandmother on the sidewalk, waving and wiping her eyes as we pulled away.

My parents had decided we would take three days to drive to Florida. "A slow drive will give us time to have fun as a family," my mother said. Three days in a car seemed long. I started worrying before we left the city. For the first hour or so, Sarai and I sat silently in the back seat. We had both grown used to living with our grandmother. The sudden move disoriented us. I knew everyone wanted to surprise us, but I wished we'd had a little more time to get used to the idea.

After a couple of hours, my mother turned the radio to a pop station instead of my father's usual classical music. Sarai and I knew the words to a lot of the songs and began to sing. Surprisingly, my parents joined in. That day and the next, our family sang. Sometimes we sang along with the radio. Other times, when we couldn't find a station, we sang whatever song one of us remembered. Our favorite was "Feeling Groovy." We must have sung it a hundred times. We sounded terrible, but I can still remember the pure joy of singing as we drove down I-95.

We stopped at almost every roadside attraction between New York and Maryland: the world's largest sheep, a two-headed calf, a rinky-dink amusement park with a Ferris wheel. At each stop, Sarai and I explored with our father while our mother stayed behind in the car with the hamsters. She kept the doors and windows open and made sure they had fresh water.

That first night, we stayed in a Howard Johnson's motel in Maryland. Even with stopping, we got there early enough to

such a pretty picture

make it to the restaurant. We'd never stayed in a HoJo's motel but we'd eaten in the restaurants dozens of times. The orange and turquoise booths and the waitresses dressed in matching uniforms felt familiar and oddly comforting. We had driven for close to eight hours without a fight or a cross word. The only hitch came when we got back to the room to get ready for bed. There were two queen beds, one with an orange bedspread and the other with a turquoise one.

"Girls, pick out a bed, and Daddy and I will take the other," my mother told us.

"You pick," I said to Sarai, hoping it would be a non-bed-wetting night.

"I want to sleep with Mommy." Sarai threw herself against our mother. We had all been doing a good job pretending everything was normal, but Sarai was done.

My mother touched my father's shoulder. "She's missed me so much." She took Sarai's hand. "You and I will sleep in the orange bed. Andrea, you'll sleep with Daddy in the blue one."

I stared at her as my chest tightened. "This room has too much orange," I said, trying to distract myself so I wouldn't cry. "It makes my head hurt."

"Andrea likes to sleep by herself on a cot," Sarai said.

I caught her eye and shook my head. I didn't want to sleep with my father, but things were going well.

"Don't act like you don't say that all the time. 'I like to sleep on my cot. Alone.'" Sarai's voice got high as she mimicked me. "She said that whenever I asked to sleep with her at Nanny's."

I chewed the inside of my mouth, worried my parents were getting mad, but they were both laughing.

"Do you want to sleep on a cot tonight?" my mother asked me. "We can put one next to the bed where Sarai and I are sleeping."

"Do they have cots here?" I asked, trying not to sound too happy.

My father shrugged. "It's HoJo's, they have everything."

Sarai smiled at me. She had saved me without knowing it. I wanted to hug her.

Fifteen minutes later, a bellman brought a folded cot to our door. To my relief, our sleeping arrangements had been decided for the rest of the trip.

We spent the next night at South of the Border, a cheesy tourist stop in South Carolina. A red banner with a painting of a mustached man in an oversized white sombrero welcomed us.

The town consisted of a couple of streets, lined with gift shops filled with faux Mexican trinkets. That afternoon, my father stayed in the motel room with the hamsters while Sarai and I explored the gift shops with our mother. When we got back, we found my father asleep on his bed, an empty bottle of gin on the nightstand next to him.

In the morning, Sarai and I, still wearing our nightgowns, stumbled out to the dark parking lot behind our parents. I fell asleep as soon as I crawled into the car. By the time I woke we were in a different parking lot.

"Where are we?" I squinted in the white sunlight. Outside, waves of heat steamed off the asphalt.

"The Dixie Diner." My mother pointed to a sign at the entrance to the lot. "Your father has a headache. He is going to take a nap while the three of us get breakfast."

The other parked cars all had Georgia license plates, so I figured we had to be somewhere in Georgia. "I'm still in my nightgown."

"I have an outfit out for each of you. You can change in the restroom."

A man in a cowboy hat got out of a red pickup. He must have noticed me watching him because he waved.

"I can't go inside wearing my nightgown," I said. "There are grown men in there. I need a coat to cover me."

such a pretty picture

"Your coats are packed. I'm not unpacking a suitcase." My mother got out of the car and opened the passenger door next to Sarai. "Besides, it's a hundred degrees out here. You'll sweat to death before you get inside."

"Please?" I knew I was causing trouble, but the idea of strange men gawking at me in my nightgown made my body itch.

My father, who had been silent up until then, got out of the car, slamming his door behind him. I clenched my fist, carving half-moons into my palms with my nails. *I should've kept my mouth shut.*

"Goddamn it, Andrea." He opened my door and bent down. His mouth was curled into a snarl and his alcohol breath felt hot on my face. He raised his hand. I braced for his slap, but just then another car pulled into the spot next to us.

My father stood up and stepped back. "Stop being such a fucking prima donna and cooperate with your mother."

Head down and face flushing with embarrassment, I followed my mother and Sarai into the diner.

That day after breakfast, no one sang. The windows were open but the silence in the car felt heavier than the air outside. I wished I could click my heels and magically arrive wherever we were going. Luckily, I fell asleep again and didn't wake up until we were almost in St. Augustine, Florida. My parents were talking in the front seat. Shutting my eyes, I stayed quiet to listen.

"I want to go straight to Winter Park," my father said.

"But we planned to spend the night here," my mother replied.

"I want this drive to be over. I feel like shit."

"That's your own fault."

"Not now, Marlene."

"The girls are having fun. There's a lot to do in St. Augustine. I want them to have a good memory of this trip."

"The fucking girls," my father grumbled. "All you care about is those goddamned girls. We should have left them with your mother permanently."

I sank deeper into my seat. My father's threats to give us away usually came after one or both of us had done something wrong. This one sounded different; it was not a threat, but instead a statement made to my mother when he thought Sarai and I were asleep. I took it as confirmation of what I already suspected that my father didn't want us and he never had.

In the end, they decided to stop in St. Augustine for a few hours. We'd save the fort and the Fountain of Youth for another time, and go to an alligator zoo on the outskirts of town. I thought it was a strange choice but Sarai was over the moon.

"Real alligators!" she hollered when we pulled into the parking lot.

Leaning over, I cupped my hands over her ear. "Daddy's still in a mood," I whispered.

My parents decided my mother wouldn't wait in the car like she usually did. We'd all go inside the zoo together. I can't remember exactly how or why this decision was made, but I'm sure it had something to do with my father's mood. Maybe my mother was afraid he'd feed one or both of us to an alligator.

"We'll leave all the windows cracked," my father told us as he poured a cup of water out of a thermos into the hamsters' tiny bowl. "They'll be fine."

The zoo reeked. In addition to alligators, there were crocodiles, lizards, snakes, and a bunch of other scaly reptiles—each one more gross than the next. I couldn't wait to leave, but Sarai loved it.

We weren't there long before my father bought himself a beer and Sarai an ice cream. He offered to buy me one too, but the smell made my stomach turn. My mother must have felt the same way, because as we walked through the zoo, she held a crumpled tissue over her nose.

such a pretty picture

The zoo had two big attractions: a snake show and an alligator show. At the snake show, when the handlers asked for a volunteer, Sarai practically jumped into the ring. The snake was twice her height and almost as thick as her body, but she laughed while the handler wrapped it around her shoulders. Then she stood smiling and petting its tail like it was one of our hamsters. By then, my father had finished his second beer and his mood had improved enough for him to let the trainers put a snake around his neck too.

At the alligator show, which we learned was actually a crocodile show, we sat in the first row and watched as the trainers put their heads into a crocodile's mouth. My mother and I squeezed each other's hands while Sarai giggled and clapped. After the show, she told us she'd been disappointed they hadn't asked for audience volunteers.

We stayed inside the zoo for a few hours. By the time we left, our clothes were damp with sweat. As we walked through the parking lot, the melting blacktop squished under my Keds. When we got to our car, my father, who had Sarai on his shoulders, handed me the keys to unlock the back passenger door. I touched the handle and pulled my hand away.

"It's too hot," I said to my mother.

She felt it and pursed her lips. "David," she said, "we need to check the back."

My father's brows furrowed. "Ange, give me the keys."

My parents walked to the back of the station wagon. Sarai and I followed.

"What's wrong?" Sarai asked me.

"Stay next to me." I grabbed her hand.

My father opened the tailgate and took out the cage. The hamsters were still.

"Are they sleeping? I want to see." Sarai tugged my hand.

"Wait." I tightened my grip.

Andrea Leeb

  My father put the cage down. My mother knelt next to it. She shook it but the hamsters didn't move. Sarai twisted her hand out of mine.
  She ran to my mother. "Mommy, why aren't they waking up?"
  My parents stood speechless. My father put his hands over his face. My mother stroked his arm.
  "What's wrong with them?" Sarai's eyes glistened. I held my breath so I wouldn't start to cry. I wanted to be strong for her but the tears came anyway.
  "Hammy, Hamlet, I'm sorry!" Sarai wailed. "It's all my fault."

chapter 13

One morning, a month after we moved into our rented townhouse, Sarai and I found our mother in the kitchen making peanut butter and jelly sandwiches. Although we'd been up for hours watching TV we were still in our pajamas.

"Andrea, do you remember where I put your lunch boxes?" she asked. We were still figuring out where things belonged. A process made harder because the townhouse was much smaller than our Oyster Bay house. At least half of our furniture ended up in storage.

"We left them at Nanny's. You said we'd get new ones." Her question confused me. Why was she worried about lunch boxes in the middle of August? We weren't supposed to start school until September. "Are we starting school today?"

"No, but we are going to my new college. I need to register for classes."

"You're going back to college?" My mother hadn't told us she was planning to go back to school.

"Your father and I think it's important I finish my degree." She pulled a silver thermos out of one of the cabinets. "Be a help and pour some apple juice into this. Do it over the sink."

"What about us?" Sarai asked, puffing her cheeks into a pout.

"I thought you two could have a picnic at the college while I register," my mother said.

Sarai stamped her foot. "I mean when you go to school."

"You'll be in school all day this year," my mother said. "And I'll only be in class two days a week."

"What if I need you?"

"I'll always be there if you need me." My mother pulled a blue-and-white striped beach bag out of a cabinet and put the thermos and the sandwiches inside of it.

"You weren't there when we lived with Nanny," Sarai said.

"Of course I was." My mother paused. "Even when you can't see me, I'm with you. Never more than a phone call away."

"Why didn't you tell us this sooner?" I asked.

"Don't start," my mother said. "Now be a good girl and help your sister get dressed."

At my mother's new college, wide paths, framed by flower beds and trees draped with Spanish moss, led between the redbrick and sun-kissed stucco buildings. The three of us walked under a sunny, cloudless sky, Sarai and I each holding one of my mother's hands. She was weighted down with the beach bag on one shoulder and an oversized purse on the other, but I noticed a lightness about her that she didn't have at home. Even her grip felt looser.

The school looked so different from the stone and sprawling ivy college my father had taught at in New York. "It's like being in a foreign land," I said.

"Some people would say we are." My mother squeezed my hand.

I laughed, although I didn't understand what she meant. It made me happy when my mother spoke to me like an adult.

"Is Daddy's new college this nice?" On the car ride over my mother had told us she wasn't going to the college where my father taught.

My mother sighed. "Daddy's teaching at a community college."

"Oh right," I said, although once again I had no idea what she meant.

such a pretty picture

She found a spot for us on the lawn in front of a yellow building, and spread out the checkered blanket we used for backyard picnics when we lived in Oyster Bay.

"I'll be in there," she said, pointing to the yellow building. "If you both stay put and eat your lunch, I'll take you for ice cream afterwards."

As she walked into the building, she blew us a kiss. After she went inside, I took out our sandwiches.

"Lunch." I held out the peanut butter with grape jelly.

"I don't want it." Sarai crossed her arms.

"I'll give you my strawberry one." My mother always made my sandwiches with strawberry jelly. I hated grape, but I wanted to keep Sarai happy and prove to my mother I could be trusted to watch her.

She shook her head. "I don't want Mommy to leave us again." Her lower lip trembled.

"She won't." I touched Sarai's hand. "She's just taking classes."

"Promise?"

"Cross my heart." I made an *x* across my chest and handed her the grape jelly sandwich. This time she took it.

We were both quiet while we ate. My father had taught at colleges for years, and between that and the peace movement, I'd spent a lot of time around college students. I liked to look at them, to pretend I was one of them. Classes hadn't started yet, but there seemed to be a lot of students around. Something about the Florida students seemed different than the students my father taught in New York. At first, I couldn't figure it out. The girls mostly had long straight hair and dressed in miniskirts, shorts, or bell-bottom jeans. There were more blondes, and I didn't see anyone dressed in black, but for the most part the Florida girls looked like the New York girls. After a few minutes I realized it was the boys who were different. In New York, most of the college boys had long hair, beards, or sideburns. The

Florida boys wore their hair much shorter; some even had crew cuts. Their faces were smooth and hairless, as if they'd just finished shaving.

My mother came back sooner than I'd expected—we'd barely finished our sandwiches. "The nice woman in charge of registration let me go to the front of the line when I explained you were waiting for me."

As we packed up our things, I pointed to a group of boys dressed in slacks and collared shirts.

"Young Republicans. This college is full of them. This whole godforsaken state is. I still can't believe we ended up here."

I watched a squirrel climbing up a Spanish moss–draped tree, while I searched for something to say to make her happy again. "Well, this college is really nice. At least you'll finish your degree someplace pretty."

She smiled. "My precocious girl, how did you get so smart?"

The following week, my mother took Sarai and me to see our new school. "It's only a few blocks away," my mother told us. "You'll be able to walk." But that day we drove.

After my mother's college, our new school seemed ugly. Concrete and dirt surrounded a single brick building, and except for one fenced-in field, there wasn't even any grass. Next to the brick building stood some kind of half-finished construction. As we walked across the parking lot to the school, we heard the sound of a jackhammer.

My mother frowned. "How are you girls going to learn in this chaos?"

As we got closer to the building, I noticed six white trailers behind it. "What are those for?" I asked.

"I guess some kind of storage," my mother said and frowned again.

such a pretty picture

~ ~ ~

Mrs. Butler, the school principal, a stout woman with a red bee-hive, sat behind a large wooden desk. "We have more students than classrooms," she said with a thick southern accent.

My mother, my sister, and I sat across from her. Three framed flags hung on the wall behind her desk. The American flag on one side, the Florida flag on the other, and a larger Confederate flag in the center. We'd seen other Confederate flags in parking lots on the drive to Florida. My parents had explained the history and what it symbolized. "Those flags represent the things Daddy and I marched against." Seeing it, I gave my mother a little kick and raised my eyes. She shook her head, letting me know to be quiet.

"What exactly does more students than classrooms mean?" my mother asked.

"It means until the addition is finished, grades four through six are in portable classrooms." Mrs. Butler stood up and walked to the window. She pointed outside to the white trailers we'd seen as we walked into the school. "Andrea, you'll be in one of those. The kids love them."

"It's so southern here," my mother said to my father that evening.

She stood in the kitchen stirring a pot of beef stew. My father leaned against the counter drinking his pre-dinner gin and tonic. In our townhouse, a long counter separated the dining room from the kitchen. I'd just finished setting the table and sat facing the kitchen, listening to my parents, hoping they'd forget about me and not force me to go into the living room where Sarai sat watching cartoons.

"That bee-hived principal has a Confederate flag hanging in her office," my mother said.

"Ignore it." My father took a sip of his drink.

"Really?" My mother stirred the stew. "What kind of message is that for our children?"

"Our children know better."

My mother walked to the refrigerator and pulled out the salad she'd made earlier. She had covered it with damp paper towels so the lettuce would keep. "What else should we ignore? Where there is racism, there is anti-Semitism. Should we ignore that too?"

"Marlene, let's not." My father finished his drink in one long swallow.

"Andrea has to go to school in a trailer."

"For God's sake, it's a portable classroom. They have them at the community college too."

"Of course they do."

My father grabbed his bottle of gin off the counter and poured himself another drink.

"Those trailers are death traps. What if there's a tornado?"

Since we'd moved, my parents fought about everything and nothing. Sometimes, it seemed like they were fighting in code. I usually kept my mouth shut but when they started talking about tornadoes, I got scared. I'd been petrified of tornadoes since the first time I saw *The Wizard of Oz*. I'd watched it several times since, and each time I had to leave the room until the tornado scene ended. "Do they have tornadoes here?" I asked.

They both stared at me. I could tell they'd forgotten I was there.

"There are no tornadoes here." My father took another sip of his drink. "This isn't Kansas."

I felt relieved; at least that was one threat I didn't have to worry about. Three months later, our neighborhood would be hit by a large tornado. One more false promise of safety in a childhood filled with my father's lies.

"No, it's not Kansas," my mother said. "It's the Jim Crow South."

"What do you want me to do? Schools weren't exactly lining up to hire me. I was lucky to get this job."

such a pretty picture

"Whose fault is that?"

"Marlene . . . stop."

"I won't. My poor girls were forced to leave their beautiful house for this godforsaken apartment. Maybe if you hadn't spent a month with that blonde, we could've saved enough to rent a real house."

"That's what you want to fight about. Still?"

"The stew is almost done." She gave the pot another stir.

"I'm doing the best I can." My father turned from my mother to me. "What are you staring at? This is your fault. If it weren't for you and your sister, none of this would've happened."

I averted my eyes. I didn't understand why he had shifted his anger from my mother to me. I wished I'd gone into the living room when I'd still had the chance.

"Look at me when I'm talking to you!"

Afraid, I kept my eyes on my plate—trying to focus on the yellow flowered pattern.

He threw the glass without warning. Like my parents' fighting, my father's temper had gotten worse in Florida. He'd spanked, slapped, and threatened us, but he'd never done anything like that before. Too shocked to duck, I watched it bounce off the edge of the table and shatter against the floor.

"David!" my mother screamed.

"What happened?" Sarai ran into the dining room.

I sat numb, still motionless.

"I've had it with this fucking family." My father stormed out of the kitchen. A few seconds later, I heard the front door slam.

"This was all my fault." My mother grabbed the dustpan and whisk broom out of the closet. I wanted her to come to me, to put her arms around me and kiss the top of my head. But she walked by me and stopped in front of the broken glass.

"He threw a glass at me."

"He didn't throw it at you. If he'd thrown it at you, it would have hit you." She wagged a finger at Sarai. "Stay put until I clean this up."

"I wasn't even doing anything."

My mother shook her head. "Your father loves you," she said as she bent down to sweep away the glass.

chapter 14

It was a Saturday in early December, and my mother had taken Sarai to a birthday party. My father and I were home alone. Dressed in shorts and a T-shirt, I lay on my bed reading *The Outsiders*. I'd checked the book out from the public library the day before. When I'd handed the librarian my library card, she'd frowned at my mother. "Don't you think she's a little young for this book? It's recommended for seventh grade and above." My mother gave the librarian one of her frosty smiles. "I'm familiar with the book but thank you for your concern." Reading it, I felt glad my mother hadn't listened. I loved it, especially Ponyboy Curtis, who I wished was real so I could fall in love with him when I became a teenager.

I always kept my door closed but not locked because my mother forbade it. "I need to get to you if there is a fire." Absorbed by my book, I didn't hear it open.

"Ange." My father's voice interrupted my reading.

He stood naked in the doorway. Closing the door behind him, he walked over to my bed and sat down next to me.

Since the day he threw the glass at me, my father's outbursts had intensified. Sarai and I treaded gingerly through each interaction, always on guard for the next violent outburst. The strange part was that as his violence intensified, my father had begun to touch me less. When he appeared in my room that day, he had not touched me for over a month. I thought it was because he hated me, that he wished my mother had left me with my grandmother, or that, like Hammy and Hamlet, I'd simply ceased to exist. Years later, I'd wonder if those months when he didn't touch me were an effort to exercise self-control or whether they were just part of my father's twisted thinking and grooming process, a Machiavellian way to teach me a lesson. In the end it didn't matter. Regardless of his underlying reasons, the impact on me was the same: At almost ten years old, I simultaneously felt relief and confusion, and began to wonder if his touch might be better than his hate and the violence that came with it.

That day, as he sat next to me, my body began to tremble. My confusion vanished. I wanted him to leave.

"Relax." He stroked my bare leg.

His fingertips felt like spiders on my skin. I wanted to smack them away but I didn't. I knew what I had to do. Shimmying out of my shorts and pink panties, I opened my legs so his spider fingers could crawl inside of me. Feeling the sting of his touch, I stared out the window at the puffy white clouds that drifted together and apart, making different shapes against the blue sky.

Focusing on clouds, I let myself fly away. Slipping through the glass like it were air, I hovered outside the window and watched the girl who was me and not me pump my father's hard penis with her hand. She worked furiously, afraid that if she did not make him come quickly there was something more he would do to her. That one day his fingers and her hand would not be enough for him. He came with a moan, and as soon as he finished, my mind joined my body. He left quickly, without telling me to keep it to myself. He knew he didn't have to.

Once he closed the door behind him, I slid off my bed and sat cross-legged on the floor. My body felt sticky from his semen. I sniffed at my hands, and the smell of him on my skin made me retch. I needed to shower. I stood up, cracked open the door, and

such a pretty picture

listened for his movements. When I heard the creak of his footsteps on the wooden staircase, I opened it a little more.

I waited a few more minutes. I didn't feel safe to move until I heard the sound of music. "The Impossible Dream"—a song from *Man of La Mancha*, the only non-opera musical my father listened to. He knew all the words and sang loudly, drowning out the record with his booming tone-deaf voice. As he played it a second time, I imagined him walking into the kitchen and pouring himself a drink. By the third time, his singing had stopped. I saw him back in the living room, sitting on his recliner, his legs stretched in front of him, a drink in his hand and a book on his lap.

I waited for the next song to finish before I tiptoed into the bathroom, locking the door behind me. I didn't care if I broke my mother's rule. Afraid he'd hear me and try to come in, my hands shook as I turned on the shower. Stepping under the hot water, I scrubbed as hard as I could. I stood there until my skin blazed red. I thought I'd gotten clean, but hours later, long after I'd dried myself off, covered my body with baby powder and changed into fresh clothing, I could still smell his stench on my skin.

Except for the first time—the time my mother went blind—my father always acted nicer after he touched me. Sunday, the next day, we went as a family to a drive-in movie. For four days, nobody got hit and nothing got thrown. That Monday, my father even came home with presents, a Barbie for me and a stuffed elephant for Sarai. "So sweet," my mother said. But I knew better. I began to convince myself that I could control my father's moods. I told myself that if I allowed him to touch me, I could make everything right. We'd never be a perfect family, but if I kept my father calm and stopped him from hitting my sister and me, it might be worth the price.

On Thursday, the fifth day, my mother defrosted two steaks for my father to barbecue on the hibachi we kept on the patio. My father taught in the morning and the early afternoon, and on Thursdays he usually got home a little after four. Plenty of time to have the steaks on the table by six thirty when the national news aired. For my father, the news was sacred. No one could talk except during commercials; even my mother had to be quiet. The Vietnam War was in full swing, the first televised war. Every night as we ate our food, we watched footage of helicopters, bleeding soldiers, and fleeing families. It made me nauseous and filled me with an ache I couldn't pinpoint.

That day, my father came home late. "I had a meeting after class," he said, walking into the dining room. I sat at the table doing my homework while Sarai colored next to me. My mother stood in the kitchen with her back to us, chopping tomatoes and cucumbers.

"How are my two girls tonight?" My father bent down between us. He smelled of alcohol and cigarettes, although neither of my parents smoked. He gave us each a sloppy kiss on one cheek. I cringed at the touch of his wet lips.

My mother turned to face us. "It's almost six," she said.

He gave her a crooked smile and walked into the kitchen. Putting his hands on her shoulders, he kissed her hello. She stepped away from him.

"Was the meeting in a bar?" she asked.

My body tensed. I poked at Sarai. "Let's go put our stuff away," I whispered.

Upstairs in our room, I kept the door open to listen for the sound of my parents fighting, but it was quiet. Still, it surprised me when less than half an hour later, my mother called us to come down for dinner.

My parents were both already sitting at the table. My father at the head and mother next to him. The portable TV had been moved from the counter to the other end of the table so my father

such a pretty picture

could see it while we ate. Sarai and I sat down at our places. Sarai next to my father and across from my mother, and me next to Sarai. My mother used a large knife to cut one of the steaks. My mother, Sarai, and I always split a steak three ways.

"The meat isn't cooked enough," my mother said.

"The steaks are fine," my father replied as David Brinkley's face flashed onto the screen. "Everyone quiet."

My mother handed me my plate. In our family we ate our meat the way my father liked it, medium-rare. But this steak looked red and bloody, rare-rare. When my mother handed Sarai her plate, she made a face. I shook my head and picked up my knife and fork. I cut a piece of meat and put it in my mouth. Barely warm. Disgusting. I wanted to spit it out but I saw Sarai watching me, so I chewed and swallowed.

Mimicking me, Sarai cut a small piece and put it into her mouth. She spit it out instantly. "I'm not eating this."

"I'm watching the news." My father scowled at her. "Eat your dinner."

"It's red." Sarai eyed my mother. "Mommy, can you make me macaroni?"

"Goddamn it." My father slammed his hand against the table. "Your mother is not making a special dinner for you. Eat what's in front of you."

I tapped Sarai's arm and put a finger against my lips. She ignored me.

"It's gross." Sarai pushed her food away.

"Shut up and eat!" My father's voice grew louder.

I stared at the TV. A group of soldiers stood in a line, unloading coffins draped with American flags from an airplane. My mother had told me the soldiers in the war were very young. "Teenagers," she'd said. Looking at the coffins, I thought about Ponyboy Curtis and wanted to cry.

"David," my mother said now, "she's seven. Go easy."

"I don't care how fucking old she is. I'm watching the news." He glared. His dark eyes narrowed and his black brows knitted together. "Eat your dinner."

"I'm not eating raw meat," Sarai cried.

"I said shut up." My father stood, towering over us.

"David, calm down." My mother got up too. He dwarfed her.

"Don't tell me to calm down. This is my house." He lifted the end of the table with both hands.

It happened fast. I jumped up, pulling Sarai with me. The table flew across the room. Dishes, glasses, silverware, and food crashed against the floor. Shards of broken glass bounced in the air like bullets. The table hit the floor facedown with a thud as the TV smashed against the wall.

"You've lost your mind!" my mother screamed.

"You fucking brat," my father yelled at Sarai, "look what you made me do."

I grabbed Sarai's arm and tried to pull her away, but she twisted out of my grip. Stepping closer to him, she put her hands on her hips. "You're the fucking brat," she said to him.

I stood stunned. Part of me wanted to put my hand over her mouth to stop her from saying more. The other part of me wished I was half as brave as she was.

"Don't you dare speak to me like that." My father slapped Sarai across the face.

She flinched and took a step back. "I hate you!" she screamed, louder this time.

"I'll show you hate." My father unbuckled his belt, but before he could get it off, my mother stepped in front of him.

"David, stop!"

I grabbed Sarai, harder this time. "Run," I said, pulling her into the hallway.

We took the stairs two at a time. Inside our room, I locked the door.

such a pretty picture

"We need to hide," I said, imagining my father kicking the door in. I thought about jumping out the window, but it was too high.

I pulled Sarai into the closet. Closing the door behind us, I piled a stack of clothes on top of us. I knew he'd be able to find us, but I wanted to make it hard for him. Sobbing, Sarai curled against me. I heard our parents' screams below us and put my hands over her head to muffle the sound. It went on for a while. Then, like the aftermath of a tornado, the house grew quiet.

"We have to stay in here," I whispered to Sarai. I'd never seen my father so angry. I sat trying not to move, terrified that he'd killed my mother and was coming for us next. My arms around Sarai, I willed her to be still. The bedroom door squeaked open and closed. I held my breath.

"Girls, it's just me." My mother opened the closet. "Daddy's asleep."

"Mommy!" Sarai fell into her arms.

"It's okay, baby." She took Sarai's hand and led her to the foot of her bed.

"How did you get in?" I asked.

"I know how to pick a lock." She held a bobby pin up for me to see. "Come sit," she said, and patted the empty spot between them.

I sat down, facing our bedroom window. While we were in the closet, the sky had darkened from pale violet to black.

My mother took my hand. "You girls need to understand that your father loves you, but he has a crazy streak."

"I'm scared of him." Sarai buried her face against my mother's shoulder.

"He doesn't mean to scare you. He can't help himself."

He'd been so angry. I studied her face. There were no bruises, at least none I could see.

"Did he hit you?" I asked.

"Daddy would never hit me."

Andrea Leeb

I pulled my hand away from hers. "But he hits us." It was a comparison I knew I wasn't supposed to make.

"Your father had a hard childhood. Someday, when you're older, I'll explain it to you. He loves you girls, he really does. We just need to do a better job of keeping him happy."

I thought about the past Saturday. How I'd let my father touch me. How I'd touched him. I clenched my hands until my nails dug into my palms. *Hadn't I made him happy? Wasn't that enough?* I wanted to tell her the truth. It would hurt her, but I didn't care. "Mommy," I said, my voice breaking.

"What, baby?" She unclenched one of my fists and kissed my open palm.

I felt an ache deep inside my chest. "We both try to be good," I said.

"We do, Mommy," Sarai said. "We really, really try to be good."

"I know you do. But we all have to try harder." She kissed the tops of our heads. "Promise me you'll both do that."

chapter 15

A few weeks before I started fifth grade, my mother walked into my bedroom. My father was at work, and Sarai was at a friend's house.

"I bought you a present." She handed me a small shopping bag.

Opening it, I pulled out a pale pink leather diary. The gift surprised me. It wasn't Chanukah or my birthday, and I hadn't asked my mother for a diary.

"You can use it instead of the yellow pads," she said.

My father kept dozens of yellow pads on his bookshelf. I used them to write stories and poems, most of which I threw away. I took them without permission. It didn't surprise me my mother had noticed, but as I ran my fingers over the diary's soft leather, I worried she might have told my father.

Watching my face, she must've read my mind. "He doesn't know."

Grateful for her silence, I kissed her cheek. "Thank you for the diary," I said.

"I bought you a pen too." She rifled through the tissue paper in the bag and pulled out a thin gold ballpoint pen. "You can pretend you're writing to a friend. Use the diary as a place to tell your secrets."

What secrets did she think I had? I ripped at a mosquito bite scab on my arm to distract myself.

My mother swatted my hand. "Don't, it will get infected."

"What if someone reads it?"

"That's what the key is for. To make sure no one reads it."

"Even you?" I was thinking this gift could be a trap.

"Even me," she said. "But I'm your mother. You can't keep secrets from me."

At first, I didn't know what to do with such a beautiful diary. I wanted the words I wrote inside of it to be beautiful too. But when I held the delicate gold pen between my fingers and tried to write about my life, I didn't have anything beautiful to say. My secrets were far too dangerous to ever put into writing. The diary needed a better owner, so I made one up: a blonde-haired, green-eyed girl named Emily. She had lots of friends, and she knew how to twirl a baton. She even sang in the school chorus with perfect pitch.

Each night after homework and dinner, I sprawled across my bed and wrote about Emily's day. I'd imagine her walking into the lunchroom, her butter-colored hair shining under the fluorescent lights. As soon as she sat down, all of the other girls rushed to sit at her table. Each night Emily's family ate dinner together. They talked about their day. No one screamed or fought, and everyone got to speak. Emily was the girl I wanted to be, with the family I wanted to have. A girl whose parents knew how to love her without causing her pain.

A few days before Valentine's Day, a month before my eleventh birthday, I woke up feeling like someone had wrapped a belt around my chest. The night before, I'd gone to bed early with a sore throat and a runny nose. I'd felt so bad, I even missed writing in my diary.

"Mommy," I tried to yell, but my voice wouldn't carry.

such a pretty picture

"Sarai," I called to my sister asleep in the next bed.

Sarai rolled over and rubbed her eyes. "Ange?"

"I'm really sick. Go get Mommy." Blinding sunlight slanted in from the bedroom window. I closed my eyes to shut it out. But instead of a soothing black, I saw red.

"Andrea." I felt my mother's cool hand against my forehead. My chest rattled each time I tried to take a breath. She helped me sit up and put two orange aspirins in my mouth. "Chew them first," she said, handing me a glass of water, "then swallow."

"Sweetheart, wake up." I heard my mother's voice. I opened my eyes and tried to focus. Both of my parents and Sarai stood above my bed. *Was it still morning? Did I have to go to school?*

"We need you to get up," my mother said. "Daddy's taking you to the hospital."

My father lifted me to a sitting position and helped me swing my legs over the edge of the bed. The room spun in circles.

My mother put a jacket around my shoulders and slipped a pair of sneakers on my feet. I felt like I was swimming underwater. Somewhere through the sound of the waves in my head, I heard Sarai crying. I wanted to tell her I was okay, but the words were too hard to speak.

My father carried me from the house to the car. He laid me in the back seat, and my mother put a pillow under my head and kissed me before we pulled away. I slept on the drive. When we parked in front of the emergency room entrance, my father lifted me out of the car. He held me close. His cheek against mine felt cool and damp.

"Don't worry," he whispered. "Daddy won't let anything bad happen to you."

I blinked open my eyes and searched his face. He'd betrayed

me so many times but at that moment I needed to believe him, to trust him. Closing my eyes again, I collapsed into his body and fell asleep.

The hours in the emergency room bubbled together. When the bubble popped, I awoke to two nurses changing me out of my nightgown into a hospital gown. My father stood at the foot of the bed. Tears streamed down his face. I tried to remember if I'd done something to make him cry.

"This will help you breathe, sugar," I heard one of the nurses say as they slipped me under a large plastic tent. Inside it was cold and damp. Misty. A soft fog cooled my hot skin. I fell back into the twilight bubble.

Two pairs of crying eyes stared down at me through the plastic. "We're here, Ange, both of us." My mother's voice. "I brought Teddy." She unzipped the tent and handed me the small brown bear I used to sleep with. I hadn't slept with him in years but he felt soft and familiar. I hugged him and fell back to sleep.

I woke again, feeling cold and wet. My mother stood next to my bed. She had unzipped the tent and slipped her hand inside.

"This gown is soaking. When was the last time you changed her?"

A nurse in a white cap and uniform stood next to her. "It's the oxygen tent, ma'am. We don't want to take her out too often."

"I brought her six brand-new nightgowns. Pretty flannel nightgowns. She's been here a week and hasn't worn one. Why do you keep putting her in those ugly hospital gowns?" My mother's voice trembled and she began to sob. Through the wrinkled plastic, I saw her chest heaving. She cradled a crumpled nightgown in her arms. "Please make her better."

Watching her through the plastic, I wanted to promise her I would be okay. But I didn't have the energy to talk. And I wasn't sure if she was really there at all.

"It's okay, honey." The nurse put her arms around my mother. "She's going to get well."

I didn't, at least not at first. I had viral pneumonia. Fluid filled my entire right lung and most of my left. As the days passed, I got sicker and sicker. I spent most of the time sedated and fevered, in and out of consciousness. Each time I woke, one of my parents sat by my side. For years, I'd remember it as proof that despite everything, they both loved me.

I felt dry and warm. The mist had evaporated. My eyes were still closed. Something covered my face. I wanted to pull it off, but my hands couldn't move. Were they tied? I heard sounds: Whoosh-whoosh-whoosh. Beep-beep-beep. The smell of rubbing alcohol permeated the air. The sheets felt itchy and rough. *Where was I?* I heard my father's voice begging me to wake up.

I woke again days later, or hours? The world around me still beeped and whooshed. *What were the sounds?* I struggled to recognize them. The whooshing reminded me of the tide: in and out. It matched my breath. The thing on my face was still there, but my hands were now free. I touched it. It felt like plastic. *Why was it there?* It blew cool air into my mouth, nose, and throat. I opened my eyes. I had dreamed I was inside a plastic tent, but the tent had disappeared.

My father stood facing me. His eyes were closed. He had a white prayer shawl draped around his shoulders. His body rocked back and forth. He spoke softly. The words sounded strange. Not

English. Hebrew. Was he praying? But my father never prayed; my father said there was no God. *Why are you praying, Daddy?* I wanted to ask, but I couldn't speak. I closed my eyes. When I opened them again, he was gone.

Dressed in a flannel nightgown and a pink fluffy robe, I walked down the hospital hallway. Holding my hand, my mother walked next to me.

"Are you okay, baby? Tell me if you need to rest."

We were heading toward the room the nurses called the sunroom. The name struck me as funny, since the room didn't have any windows except the ones facing the hallway. I guessed that the room got its name because the walls were painted bright yellow.

By then, I had been in the hospital for twenty-three days. My lungs were clear and my fever had finally broken. The doctor had told me if I stayed fever-free for two more days, I could go home. When I promised him that I'd try my best, he laughed. But I'd meant it. As much as I feared my father and the chaos of our house, I wanted to go home. I missed my room, my books, and most of all I missed my sister. Because of hospital rules, I hadn't seen her since I'd been admitted. Feeling better, I worried about her. My mother had assured me she was okay, but my mother saw the world the way she wanted to see it. The only thing that alleviated my fear was the knowledge that a few days after I went into the hospital, my grandmother had come to stay with my family. "It's so cute," my mother said. "Nanny sleeps in Sarai's bed because Sarai insists on sleeping in yours. She even wears your nightgowns to sleep in."

From the hallway, I noticed two people sitting on the couch. Before I took a step inside, I heard Sarai call my name. "Ange!" She barreled into me, almost knocking me over. I buried my face in her honey waves, inhaling the smell of Prell shampoo and sweat.

such a pretty picture

"*Mamaleh*, I came to visit many times but you were always asleep." Nanny stood behind my sister. Sarai let me go so my grandmother could get closer. She kissed my face and held me. Her body felt soft and warm. She smelled like rose water and butterscotch candy, her signature scent. She stepped back and took my hands in hers. "You've gotten so skinny. We need to get you home and fatten you up."

"How did you get permission?" I asked my mother. I had been begging her to sneak Sarai in since I'd started feeling better, but my mother hated to break rules.

"The head nurse, but only for thirty minutes." My mother tapped on her watch. "Nanny and I will wait in your room for a little while so you two can visit alone. We'll be right down the hall if you need us."

Sarai and I sat next to each other on the butter-colored couch. On the wall across from us, someone had painted a mural of multicolored balloons.

"I missed you so much," she said. "I thought you were going to die—to leave me."

"You can't get rid of me." I tickled her stomach.

"I was so scared." Her chocolate eyes welled.

"I'm fine now," I said. "I'll be home soon." She burrowed into me. I inhaled the scent of her again. "Has everything been okay at home? With Daddy?"

"He wasn't home much. When he was, he mostly slept and cried. He loves you."

I nodded, not sure what to say.

"I brought some of your things." She grabbed a shopping bag that my grandmother had left on the far end of the couch. "I didn't know what book you wanted, but this one seemed good." She handed me *The Secret Garden*. When I was about five, the book had been one of my favorites. I still read it to Sarai on the nights when my parents fought more than usual or when she couldn't fall asleep. "And I brought your diary."

Handing the diary to me, she studied me as if she were waiting for me to get angry. The gold key was inside the lock.

"How'd you find the key?"

I kept the diary in my underwear drawer. It would have been easy for her to find, but I'd hidden the key inside a pair of rolled-up pink-and-white striped knee socks. She must've ransacked my whole dresser to find it.

She shrugged without answering.

"Did you read it?"

"No." Eyes down, she pointed the toes of her white Keds and made little circles on the floor.

"You're lying." I laughed. I'd missed her so much, nothing could make me mad at her.

Hearing me laugh, she looked up. "Who's Emily?"

"She's make-believe."

"I thought a diary is supposed to be about your life."

"Mine is fiction," I said, thinking how disappointed she must have been reading it. "It's more fun making things up. Better than real life."

Sarai nodded, her eyes welling with tears again.

I stroked her hand. "I can't wait to come home."

"Am I Amy?" she asked, referring to Emily's little sister. I'd named her after the youngest sister in *Little Women* although I had made my Amy less bratty than the Amy in the book.

"Yes."

She smiled. "Good. Amy is nice. And fun."

"Emily loves Amy." I wrapped my arms around my sister.

chapter 16

A few months later, on the morning of my mother's graduation, she stood dressed in a half-slip and bra studying her reflection in the mirrored closet. She held up a yellow dress and then a navy one. Sarai and I sat on the bed. My father was downstairs drinking his coffee and watching *Meet the Press*.

"Wear your yellow dress," I said.

"I was going to wear the blue one."

"The yellow is prettier."

My father had ordered a bouquet of pale-yellow roses, my mother's favorite. "It has to be our secret," my father told me, and I had smiled. For once, we had a secret I was happy to keep.

"I don't know what I'm carrying on about. The dress is going to be hidden under my gown."

"You'll take the gown off after, when we go to dinner. If you wear the yellow Sarai and I can wear our yellow dresses too."

"If we all match, everyone will know we're your daughters," Sarai added.

"Good thinking," I said, glad she'd gone along with me. She didn't know about the roses.

"Sarai can't be trusted to keep a secret from your mother," my father had told me.

"The yellow it is." My mother hung up the navy dress and slipped the yellow one over her head. "I can't believe I'm graduating.

I would have never been able to do it if I didn't have such wonderful daughters." She smiled and opened her arms wide.

While she finished dressing, she explained to us that we were all going to the graduation, but she had to be there earlier than the rest of us.

"Daddy will take me and come back. That way, you don't have to sit in the heat for so long." She put a hand on each of our shoulders. "This is an important day for me. Promise you won't fight with your father."

We both promised, but I felt a little sick. My father's temper had improved, but there were still times when the smallest mistake caused him to explode. I felt like it was up to me to keep the peace, and make sure all three of us behaved.

My mother didn't have to tell me how much graduation meant to her. I already knew. A month before, she'd told me she'd never expected to go to college. We were both sitting at the dining table. I'd been too weak when I got home from the hospital to go back to school and had spent the rest of the year on home study. My mother and I got in the habit of doing our homework together. That day, we were both working on papers: mine on US history and hers on Russian literature. I started the conversation because my mother loved books as much as I did, and I didn't understand why she'd gotten married right after she finished high school.

"Why didn't you go to college first?" I asked her, pushing my history book away.

"You know how Nanny is. Girls are supposed to get married and have babies. Period."

"But Uncle Matt went to college."

"Uncle Matt is a man."

I nodded. My grandmother had never stopped bugging my mother about going back to school. She'd made it clear she thought it was a waste of time and money.

such a pretty picture

"The truth is, I didn't think I was smart enough back then. Everyone always told me I was pretty, but nobody ever said I was smart."

This revelation astonished me. I thought about how many books my mother read and how she had told me that for her books were like air; how she got almost all As in school, set up antiwar protests, and still managed to take care of all of us. My mother was the smartest woman I knew.

"I wouldn't have gone to school at all if I hadn't married your father. He was the one who suggested it."

"Really?" I was surprised, although my mother had always told me that the thing that set my father apart from other boys she had dated was his love of books. The father I knew treated my mother like a servant.

"He was the first person to tell me I was smart. He gave me confidence. He rescued me. If I hadn't married him, I would've been stuck in the Bronx forever."

Driving to the college on the way to the graduation, I realized that my mother must have also told my father not to fight with us. Everyone was on their best behavior, and we made it out of the house and into the car without a single moment of tension. He even bought Sarai and me each a white balloon when we stopped at the florist to pick up the roses.

At the college, rows of folding chairs had been set up on the main lawn. They were divided into two sections, with a long plastic carpet running down the middle. In front of the chairs was an empty stage with a microphone, and behind the microphone several rows of chairs.

We were twenty minutes early but there were already a lot of people sitting.

"Look, empty seats." Sarai pointed to the first five rows.

My father put his hand on her shoulder. "Those are for the

graduates." He bent down next to her. "See the ones on the stage? Those are for the faculty."

"Is that where you sit when your students graduate?" Sarai asked.

"Yes, that's where I sit." My father stood and rubbed her head. "We need to find three seats together on an aisle so Daddy can stretch his legs."

The seats we found were twenty rows back.

"But we won't be able to see Mommy," Sarai said.

I twitched. Everything was going so well, I didn't want her to make my father angry.

"Sit next to me, and I'll lift you up so you can see her," he said.

I relaxed.

"Put these under your seat so they don't wilt." My father handed me the roses.

Once we sat down, I tied one balloon to my wrist, and the other to Sarai's. "So they don't blow away," I said, and paused. "If you need anything, tell me, not Daddy."

I had never been to a graduation before. I turned my head every so often as the rows behind us filled with people. I didn't see any children, although my mother had told me she was not the only mother graduating. Wondering if their parents had made them stay home, I felt lucky to be included.

"How long?" Sarai asked me after a few minutes.

I had gotten a watch for Chanukah, a Timex with a thin black band. Except when I was in the hospital, I wore it all the time, even to sleep. Knowing the time gave me a feeling of control. "Only ten more minutes," I said, looking at my watch. "Do you want to play tic-tac-toe?"

I had brought my straw purse with me. Other than school, I never went anywhere without a purse, although they were usually empty. That day, I'd stuck some tissues and a small notepad and a pencil inside. Exactly like my mother would have.

such a pretty picture

The graduation began with a song called—my father would tell us at dinner—"Pomp and Circumstance." On the first note, everyone stood. In procession, the faculty walked down the plastic carpet and made their way onto the stage. The graduates followed. My father picked up Sarai and let me stand in front of him.

"Mommy!" Sarai and I yelled together as my mother passed us. She waved and blew us a kiss.

Florida was always hot in late May, but that day the sun felt unrelenting. Dressed in a mini, my bare thighs stuck to the wooden chair. On top of the heat, the speeches droned on forever. I watched the adults around me fidget in their seats like kindergartners. The woman sitting next to me took out her compact and reapplied her lipstick three times. Her husband sat reading the newspaper, and the man next to him held a transistor radio against his ear.

"They must be hot in those gowns," Sarai whispered to me.

Earlier, I'd given her my pad and pencil to draw and it struck me that my eight-year-old sister might have been the best-behaved person in our entire section. My mother would have been proud of her.

"Good thing Mommy never sweats." I fanned her face with the commencement program.

"Not like Daddy." She pointed to his armpits, which were already wet.

My mother had laid out an extra shirt for him to change into before we went to dinner. I was glad I had reminded him to bring it.

Finally, after fifty-five minutes, the students began to receive their diplomas in alphabetical order.

"Your mother is up soon," my father said as they started awarding diplomas to students whose last name began with the letter L. He picked Sarai up. "Stand on your chair," he said to me.

I hesitated, feeling funny about the people behind me. Then I remembered my conversation with my mother in the dining room—how she told me she didn't think she was smart. Even if it made other people angry, I had to see her take her diploma. Peering over a sea of heads, I watched as my mother walked on stage. My heart raced, not in a bad but in a joyful way. As the dean presented her diploma, I cheered wildly, surprising my sister and father. I'd never felt so proud to be her daughter.

Afterward, the green lawn and the walkways were crammed with families and graduates hugging and taking pictures.

"There she is," my father said, pointing to a large leafy tree.

Sarai and I pushed through the crowd until we got close enough to see her. She had opened her gown and her bright yellow dress peeked out between the black folds. She still had her cap on, and her face was flushed from the excitement and the heat of the summer sun.

"Mommy!" Sarai and I shouted.

We ran to her, our white balloons still attached to our wrists floating above us.

"My girls." She enfolded us into her gown.

My father stood behind us, holding the yellow roses.

I took Sarai's hand. "Let Daddy have a hug," I said, taking a step back.

"I'm so proud of you, pussycat." My father handed her the roses and kissed her. Yellow petals fluttered to the ground, and they kissed again, a long deep kiss, like the kind I'd seen in movies.

Then holding hands, they turned to face us. With her bouquet in her right hand and her left clasping my father's, my mother reminded me of a black-gowned bride. Her gold wedding ring glinted in the sunlight. My eyes fell on my father's left hand. His fingers were empty—no wedding ring, not even the shadow of a tan line. I wondered how long it had been missing

such a pretty picture

and what that meant, but before I had a chance to process it, my mother smiled.

"Except for the day I married your father this has been the best day of my life. Thank you girls for being so good." Then she turned to my father and kissed him again. "And thank you for everything. I love you."

Part Two
1969-1981

chapter 17

After noticing my father's missing wedding ring, I spent the summer alternately looking forward to and dreading what I'd decided was my parents' impending divorce. It didn't happen; the only big change was another move a few weeks before the end of summer vacation. My father had been promoted to associate chairman of the English department at his college and received a contract from a large publishing company to write a political science textbook. With his promotion, the book, and my mother's new job teaching first grade, we had enough money to move out of the townhouse and rent a real house. Our new place was in Maitland, not Winter Park, which meant we'd have to change schools again. I was going into sixth grade; this new school would be my fifth one since kindergarten.

In the new house, Sarai and I each had our own room. At eleven, having my own room didn't make me nervous in the same way it had when I was younger. My father had stopped touching me after I got sick. I hoped it was over for good—that he'd keep whatever promise he'd made that night in the hospital—but I knew if he began again, it would have nothing to do with whether or not I had my own room. I'd begun to understand that my father believed he owned me. I was his to do with as he pleased.

We were in the new house for only a month when he started up again. He never came at night; instead, he waited for those weekend days when my mother and sister were out. He had ample opportunity. At our new school, as in our last one, Sarai made friends easily. She'd also joined Brownies, and my mother had agreed to be a troop leader. Although I wasn't a target, I didn't have many friends. I still spent most of my time at home reading or writing stories about Emily and her family.

By then, I knew that what my father and I were doing was wrong. I'd always known it, but I never really understood why. In sixth grade, my understanding of my relationship with my father shifted. Some of it had to do with the kids at school. On the playground and at lunch they were starting to talk more about kissing, periods, and—although we didn't have formal sex education—sex. And then, probably more importantly, there were the books.

I already read above my grade level, but after I got sick, I started reading adult books, the kind taught in high school or college. My parents kept a collection of classics in my father's study. At least a hundred books covered in a rust-colored material. Over the years, I'd studied the bindings of the books, tracing my fingers over the engraved gold titles, but I'd never worked up the courage to take one off the shelf. During the previous spring, my mother had given me *Pride and Prejudice*. She'd been too busy finishing her senior thesis to take me to the library, and because I had not returned to school, I couldn't get books on my own. I loved it. When I finished, I asked if I could take another. My mother surprised me by saying yes. "Read what you want so long as you take care of the books and you don't go into the office when your father is in there." By the time I started sixth grade, I'd finished *Jane Eyre* and *Anna Karenina*.

When I showed my mother *Jane Eyre*, she had smiled and told me to enjoy it. But a few weeks later, when I picked out *Anna Karenina*, she almost stopped me. "That's too complicated for you."

"But it's one of your favorites," I whined, refusing to let go of the book.

Andrea Leeb

After a few days, I wore her down. I'd discover she was right about the book's complexity; there was a lot I didn't understand, and I skimmed whole chapters. But Anna's doomed relationship with Vronsky gave me my first glimpse into adult passion—it showed me how destructive and obsessive love could be. And although the book did not directly pertain to me, on some indirect level it made me realize how twisted the things my father did to me were. It's hard to recall exactly why my prepubescent mind drew that particular connection, but that summer crystalized a level of awareness that I'd not had before. And although I am sure my father did not know the exact reason why, he knew I had changed.

The way he treated me changed too. His threats became clearer. "If you ever tell, no one will believe you over me," he'd say. "And if I do find out, I will put you away. Forever." At the same time, he began to manipulate me and pay attention to me in other ways. He started to comment on my looks. He no longer told me I was cute. "You're turning into a beautiful woman," he'd say instead. "And sexy. You remind me of a young Sophia Loren." He even showed me a picture of her so I could see what he meant. When he'd say things like that to me, I liked it. I wanted my father to think I was beautiful. And although I still had a somewhat foggy understanding of what it meant to be sexy, I even wanted him to think I was sexy. But mostly, despite my fear and disgust, I ached for his love. I hated myself because of it, but there was a part of me that was willing to do almost anything to get it.

One Saturday in early November, my father and I were home alone. He'd already been in my room, and I had showered and changed. By then, the touching had taken on a warped normalcy. I no longer shook in terror when he showed up. My fear had been replaced with shame, and I'd begun to find ways to deal with it.

such a pretty picture

❦ ❦ ❦

That day, I'd used my mother's tweezers to pull out my leg hairs one by one. I was up to twenty. It hurt, but the pain always made me feel a little bit better. I'd just finished plucking the last hair when I heard a knock at my door. My body tensed. My father had never touched me twice in the same day, but there were no rules.

"Ange." My father knocked again.

I shut my eyes as I cracked the door. When I opened them, he stood in the hallway wearing a white collared polo shirt and mustard polyester bell-bottom pants. My mother hated the color of those pants. Seeing him fully dressed, I felt lightheaded with relief.

He gave me one of his charming smiles. "I want to take you shopping for a new outfit."

I opened the door wider. "Is Mommy home?" Over the years, my father had given me gifts afterward, but he'd never taken me shopping.

"I want it to be the two of us."

My shoulders tensed again. I loved to shop, but I shopped with my mother. It was one of the special things we did together. I didn't want to do it with my father, but I didn't want to make him angry either.

"Come on, cutie, give your old man the pleasure of buying you something pretty."

Outside the air felt hot and sweaty, more like August than November. Dressed in white shorts and an embroidered peasant blouse, I sat next to my father in the front seat of his car. My legs were shaking, but he didn't seem to notice. He clicked on the radio—as always, the classical music station—and hummed along with the symphony. I opened my window and let the warm, humid air wash over me.

He took me to Jordan Marsh, which my mother said was the Florida version of Macy's but better. Since moving to Florida, our family always shopped there. Walking inside, the air-conditioning hit me with an icy blast. I thought about how my mother would have made me bring a cardigan or jacket.

He must have thought of her, too, because he touched my arm before we even took two full steps. "I left your mother a note, telling her I took you shopping after losing a bet to you."

He had to be kidding. "Really?" I looked at him cross-eyed.

"It's after two. They might get home early." He smiled. "So . . . what did we bet on?"

I put my hair into my mouth, something I had stopped doing over the past year. I sucked on it hard. I wanted to go home.

"Well?" He studied me, waiting for an answer.

I was stuck for a moment, then had an idea. "You bet me I couldn't name the six wives of Henry the Eighth."

My parents had recently taken Sarai and me to see the movie *Anne of the Thousand Days*. Sarai was too young for the movie and hated it, but I'd loved it. After we got home, I'd read about all of the wives in the encyclopedia and begged my mother to buy me a book about them.

"That's a good one," he chuckled.

He took my hand and led me to the escalator. I flinched from his touch. "Can you name them—the six wives? In case your mother asks."

My stomach twisted into a knot. "Yeah, I can."

"*Yes*, not *yeah*," he corrected me.

The Junior Girls department was on the third floor. I'd begun to shop there the month before, having gained back most of the weight I'd lost when I was sick. The first time my mother took me, I'd been thrilled. But that day, as I stood next to my father, watching him rifle through the racks of clothing, his long fingers touching the hanging pastel dresses, the tuna sandwich I'd had for lunch rose into the back of my throat and I had to fight the urge to vomit.

such a pretty picture

He picked out three minidresses: a paisley lavender with a matching scarf, a pink with white piping on the neck and sleeves, and a silky one with navy and white stripes. Pretty dresses, but the tuna rose up again at the thought of trying them on.

A brassy-haired saleswoman, wearing a tight minidress, made a beeline for us. She appeared to be about my mother's age, and as she walked toward us, I noticed she had a roll in her middle and dimples on her knees.

"My daughter would like to try these on." My father handed her the dresses.

"What a lucky girl." She smiled at me, and then gave my father a longer smile. I hoped he wouldn't mock her on our drive home.

I followed the saleslady into the dressing room. "Your daddy has good taste," she said as she hung up the clothes.

My father had never shopped with me, but when we'd lived in New York he often shopped with my mother. "Your father has the best taste," she'd tell me while I sat on my parents' bed watching her open shopping bags of clothes from Bonwit Teller or Saks.

Standing in the dressing room, the saleslady smiled at me again. I could tell she was waiting for me to react. "My mother says that too." I forced myself to smile.

My father sat on an oversized leather chair in a small area outside of the dressing room. The beaming saleslady stood next to him while I, following my father's instructions, twirled and primped like a beauty queen. For a moment, the knots in my stomach loosened as I allowed myself to bask in his attention. I felt beautiful. Not just beautiful; I felt loved. In the end, after I tried on all of the dresses, he decided on the lavender paisley with the matching scarf.

"You can wear this around your waist, your neck, or like a headband." The saleslady showed me how to wrap the scarf around my hair. Then she grabbed a pair of oversized white sunglasses off of a mannequin and put them on my face. "You look like a movie star," she said, and smiled at my father.

"My little Sophia Loren." My father winked at me. "We'll take that dress and the sunglasses too."

Looking at him, I blushed, although I wasn't sure if it was from shame or pride.

chapter 18

A black cloud sucks me up. The wind howls. It sounds like a freight train running through my brain. I spin in circles as the wind rips at my arms and my legs. The endless cloud twists and turns. There is no sunlight, only blackness and more blackness. Someone screams.

I woke to the sound of my own screaming. No longer spinning, I felt my bare feet planted firmly on the floor. A light hit my eyes. I blinked and blinked again. I saw my family standing in the hallway. They were all dressed for bed, my mother in her nightgown, Sarai in her pajamas, and my bare-chested father in his shorts. Sarai clutched her Snoopy Dog in one hand and clung to my mother's nightgown with the other. I heard my mother's voice but couldn't make out what she said. My ears still rang with the sound of my screams. I stared at my family. *How did I get here? And why were they there?*

My mother moved toward me. She touched my face. Her fingers felt cool against my warm skin.

I blinked again. "Am I awake or asleep?"

"You're safe," she reassured me. "It was just a bad dream."

She took one of my hands and motioned for my sister to take the other. Together, they led me back to my bed.

I'd had nightmares before, but not like that, and I'd never

walked in my sleep. I hoped it wouldn't happen again, but it did, with two alternating dreams: the tornado and the tidal wave. Different events, but the same feeling, the same fear, and the same sleepwalking. At first, the nightmares happened only on the days my father touched me. But after a few weeks they became more frequent. It didn't matter whether he touched me or not. By Christmas, I had the dreams every night.

On a Sunday in February, a month before my twelfth birthday, my mother shook me awake. Startled, I clenched my jaw and kept my eyes shut tight.

"Sarai just left to go horseback riding with Sandy and her mother. Daddy and I need to talk to you while she is out."

"In here?" I sat up. The idea of my parents being in my room at the same time panicked me.

"In the nook. Daddy's making eggs."

"Am I in trouble?"

"We'll talk during breakfast."

I dragged myself out of bed. Whatever they wanted to talk to me about couldn't be good, if they had to do it while Sarai was out. Taking my time, I washed my face, brushed my teeth, and changed into a pair of shorts and a T-shirt. As I dressed, I tried to figure out what I had done wrong. The thought crossed my mind that my father might have confessed, but it lasted only a second. No way. That was one thing I felt certain he'd never do.

The nook was an alcove off the side of the kitchen. Big enough for a round table, four chairs, and a stand for our portable TV, we ate most of our meals there. By the time I walked in, my parents were already eating.

"We were wondering what took you so long," my mother said.

The smell of the food made me gag, but I pretended to be hungry and put a scoop of scrambled eggs and a strip of bacon

such a pretty picture

on my plate. For a few minutes we sat without talking. Pushing my eggs around my plate, I began to think they'd changed their minds about whatever they needed to discuss with me.

My father took another piece of bacon and more eggs. My mother moved her plate away and put her napkin on the table. She hadn't touched her food either.

"We need to talk about the nightmares," she said.

I slunk down in my chair. "I don't have them on purpose."

"I know you don't, but no one is getting any sleep, and you're scaring your sister."

"Scaring is an understatement," my father said. "Sarai is terrified of you."

My armpits tingled and my face grew hot. "It's not my fault." I fought the impulse to run back to my room.

"We know that, sweetheart," my mother said.

"You're disrupting the whole family," my father said.

Bile burned the back of my throat. I swallowed it, then asked, "Are you going to send me away?"

"Oh God," my mother gasped. "Why would you say that?"

I stared at my father. Refusing to meet my eyes, he stood up with his coffee cup in one hand. "More coffee, Marlene?" He grabbed her cup and walked into the kitchen before she answered.

My mother pursed her lips. "We're worried about you." She took my hand. "We found a doctor we'd like you to talk to," she said, stroking my hand.

I pulled my hand away. "You think I need to see a shrink?" It was a word I'd heard on some TV show, probably *Bewitched* or *I Dream of Jeannie*. It had been used in a joke about crazy people.

"He's a psychiatrist. He specializes in helping children and teenagers."

"When do I have to go?" Maybe I had time to get them to change their minds.

"Soon. He told us to tell you first, to give you time to get used to the idea."

I dug my nails into my palms, wishing they were long enough to make me bleed. "You already met with him?"

"He's very nice," my mother said.

"Did you meet with him too?" I asked my father as he sat back down.

"We wouldn't put you into therapy without both of us talking to the doctor first."

"I don't even know what therapy is."

"We don't want you to be upset," my mother said.

"What did you tell him?" My leg shook so hard the table began to vibrate.

"This is a good thing, not a bad thing," she said, avoiding my question.

"Tell me what you told him." I directed the request to my father.

"That you need professional care. That you're hysterical, and that we are not equipped to deal with your problems."

"You told him I'm crazy." I thought about *Jane Eyre* and Rochester's wife. Was I going to end up locked away in an attic too?

"Disturbed," my father said.

"We want you to get well." My mother held out her hand, but I refused to take it.

"I'm not crazy. I don't need help." I wanted to throw my plate against the wall the way my father did when he got mad, but I stopped myself. It would only prove their point. Instead, I stood up. And without saying another word, I ran out of the room.

"Ange." They both called for me.

"We love you," I heard my mother's voice implore. "Don't be angry. Come back."

I didn't turn around. They'd already decided on the story. There was nothing more for us to talk about.

such a pretty picture

Sarai and I usually got home from school about an hour before my mother. Every day, I'd make us both a snack, and we'd sit together watching *The Dating Game* and *Gilligan's Island* reruns while we waited for our mother. Sarai didn't like coming home to an empty house, but I loved it. It was the one time of day I didn't have to be worried.

On Monday, the day after the talk, when Sarai and I got home, both cars were parked in our driveway. Our parents stood at the front door waiting for us. Sarai went right to my mother for a hug, but I stood back. My mother was dressed as usual in one of her teacher outfits—a blouse, a knee-length skirt, and pumps. But my father, who usually wore a shirt and a pair of slacks to work, was wearing a suit and tie.

"Are you going on a trip?" I asked my father. He hated ties, and he wore suits only when he traveled up north to meet with the publishing company.

"No, I am taking you to the doctor."

"I'm going to the doctor today?"

"We told you that yesterday," my mother said.

"You said soon. You said you were giving me time to get used to it." I dropped my book bag on the floor with a thud. "You didn't say today."

"Calm down," my father said.

My head throbbed. "Are you both taking me?"

"Just your father," my mother said.

"I want you to take me," I said to her.

"I am staying here with Sarai. Daddy came home early to take you."

I thought again about Rochester's wife. My father never came home early, and except for the time he took me to the hospital, he never took me to the doctor. He was doing it now on purpose.

116

He wanted me to be afraid. He wanted to make sure everyone thought I was crazy.

"Come on, cutie. If we leave now, we can stop for a chocolate shake on the way." He smiled at me.

I looked at the slanted chip in his front tooth. I had always thought the chip was cute, but that moment, I hated it. I hated his smile. But most of all, I hated him.

"I don't want a chocolate shake, and I need to change before we go," I said, and picked up my book bag.

Alone in my room, I pulled out the paisley lavender mini-dress my father had bought me on our shopping trip. I'd worn it only once, a couple weeks after I got it. We were all going to a restaurant and my mother had suggested I wear it. "You'll make your father happy," she'd said. During dinner, both of my parents made a big deal about how pretty I looked. At first their compliments made me feel good, but then I began to feel guilty. Ashamed. When we got home, I had to poke myself with a pin fifty times to feel better.

That afternoon, I put on the lavender dress. I wasn't sure why I wanted to wear it, but I knew it wasn't to make my father happy. Once I'd changed, I wrapped the matching scarf around my hair like a headband—exactly the way the saleslady had shown me. I studied my reflection in my closet door mirror. The dress was pretty, but except for my dark hair and eyes and my olive complexion, I didn't look anything like Sophia Loren or any other movie star. All I could see was a scared almost-twelve-year-old girl. A girl who didn't know how to protect herself from the people who supposedly loved her. I stood for a few minutes looking at that girl in the mirror and wondered what I needed to do to make sure she survived.

chapter 19

On the drive over to Dr. W's office, my father and I didn't speak. At first, I'd expected him to lecture me, to tell me to keep my big mouth shut, but as we drove it dawned on me that he knew it wasn't necessary. Confident that he'd taught me well, my father knew I understood that silence was my only choice.

As an adult, I'd wonder why my parents risked sending me to a psychiatrist. While it's true that things were different back then, it seems like a crazy decision. Even for my parents. Over the years I've hoped that it was my mother's idea. A message to my father that she knew about the abuse and wanted it to stop. But she'd never said, and the few times I tried to ask her she changed the subject. Then again maybe it was my father's idea, an attempt to get me to believe that I was disturbed. A hysterical little girl. The family's identified patient.

That day we arrived at Dr. W's office fifteen minutes early. The waiting area, a windowless room with a tan couch and two matching chairs, had a closed door on one wall, which I figured led into the doctor's real office. A woman with short blonde hair and pearls sat in one of the chairs reading a magazine.

"Take a seat." My father pointed to the couch and sat down on the empty chair.

Andrea Leeb

I grabbed a magazine off the coffee table, something called *Field & Stream*. When I realized it was a camping magazine, I didn't want to draw attention to myself by putting it back and trying to find another. As the minutes crept by, I sat with it on my lap pretending to read an article about fly fishing. I heard my heart beating: *thump, thump, thump*. It reminded me of an Edgar Allan Poe story we'd read in school; I had my very own tell-tale heart. I glanced at my father and the blonde woman to see if they heard it too, but they both sat absorbed by, or pretending to be absorbed by, their magazines.

Finally, after what felt like forever, the door to the doctor's office opened and a blonde girl with shoulder-length hair walked out. Probably a year or two older than me, she wore a gray corduroy skirt and a tight pink sweater. A thick silver ID bracelet that must have belonged to her boyfriend dangled on her wrist. She looked like the type of girl who was popular, not crazy. The blonde woman stood up and, without talking, the two of them left the waiting room.

Alone with my father, I kept my eyes glued to my magazine. After a couple more minutes, the door to the inner office creaked open. A short balding man with gold wire-frame glasses stepped out. He was dressed in black slacks and a wrinkled white shirt. *Schlump*, my mother would have said. My father stood up and adjusted his suit jacket. Looking down at the man, he extended his hand.

I sat watching them without moving, not sure what I should do.

"You must be Andrea," the man said to me.

I jumped up and my magazine fluttered to the floor. Flustered, I bent down to pick it up. When I stood up, my father looked irritated, but the man gave me a sympathetic smile.

"I'm Dr. W," he said, and motioned for me to come into the other office.

My father and I followed, but before we walked inside, Dr. W stopped. "Just Andrea," he said to my father.

such a pretty picture

I flinched. My father's eyes narrowed. I wondered if Dr. W could tell he was annoyed. Still, he returned to the waiting area without saying anything as I went with the doctor.

The inside office didn't have any windows either, but it felt more open than the waiting room. Pictures of sailboats and seashells hung on the wall. In the center of the room, a light-blue fabric couch sat across from a black leather chair and a side table. In the far corner, I noticed a child-sized table, two small chairs, and an open toy box filled with stuffed animals. I shuddered, remembering how I wanted to die when I was a little girl.

"Have a seat on the couch." Dr. W sat down in the leather chair and took a yellow pad and pen from the side table.

He asked me some questions about myself, simple questions like my grade and my hobbies. "Reading and writing stories," I said. My favorite subject at school? "A three-way tie between English, history, and civics. Anything but math." He asked if I played any sports. "Not at school, but I like to roller-skate."

"Do you have any questions for me?"

"What am I supposed to do in therapy?" I had never gotten a direct answer from my parents.

"All you have to do is talk."

I studied my shoes. I had worn my white go-go boots. My feet had grown recently and the boots pinched my toes, but they looked good with the lavender dress. I noticed a smudge on the left toe, so I crossed my right leg over my left, hoping Dr. W wouldn't see it.

"Do you like to talk?" he asked me.

"My father says I talk too much. That I'm self-centered." I blushed. I'd never been alone in a room with a strange man before. I thought about my father. If anything happened, I knew he'd rescue me. No one was allowed to hurt his daughters. Except him.

"Is there anything else you want to know?"

I stared past him at the overflowing toy box. I didn't trust adults and I had no reason to trust Dr. W. "If I talk to you, tell you things, will you tell my parents?"

"Our conversations are confidential. Do you know what that means?"

"Secret. Between you and me." I paused. "So . . . no matter what I tell you, you'll keep it a secret?"

"Yes, for the most part," he said. "There are a few things that I can't keep secret."

"What things?" I stared at the thick lenses in Dr. W's glasses. I had recently started wearing glasses for seeing the blackboard and watching movies. I hated them but at least my lenses weren't as thick as Dr. W's.

"If you tell me you are planning to do something dangerous or hurt yourself, then I would need to tell your parents."

"You mean like Anna?"

"Who?"

"Anna Karenina. She loved Vronsky. She gave up her son for him, but Vronsky didn't love her as much as she loved him. She was so heartbroken that she threw herself in front of a train. It was the saddest book I ever read."

"You read *Anna Karenina*?"

"I read all kinds of books." My parents hated it when I bragged, but I couldn't help myself. "I read *Pride and Prejudice* and *Jane Eyre*, too, and I just started *Vanity Fair*."

He wrote something on his pad. I felt like I had surprised him. It made me feel more in control, but also a little disappointed. That he didn't already know how much I read meant my parents hadn't thought it was important enough to tell him. They'd probably only told him the bad things about me: my problems, my nightmares, and my tears. "She's disturbed. She's destroying our family." I imagined my father saying these things as my mother sat next to him, holding his hand and nodding in agreement.

such a pretty picture

"Anna is a good example," he said after he'd finished writing. "If you told me you were planning to kill yourself or hurt yourself like Anna did, I would need to tell your parents."

"Don't worry, I'm nothing like Anna." I decided not to tell Dr. W about sticking myself with pins. How each time I did it, I added another five pricks. Or how I plucked my leg hairs to make myself hurt. And I'd never mention my five-year-old suicide attempt. None of those things were dangerous, anyway. Besides, it was my mother, not me, who reminded me of Anna. Like Anna and Vronsky, my mother was willing to sacrifice anything to make my father happy. Even though my parents fought a lot, I knew my mother couldn't live without him. I worried about what she'd do if he ever stopped loving her or started loving someone else more. Or if she ever found out about the way my father "loved" me.

"I'm glad to hear that. But I want you to tell me if you ever feel that sad."

"Is there any other reason you'd tell my secrets?"

"If I thought another person was doing something to hurt you." I furrowed my brow. "Like if a neighbor hit me?"

"That's one example," he said and paused. "Has that happened?"

"No, not a neighbor," I said, immediately regretting my answer. Knowing I had made a mistake, I waited for him to ask the next question. *Has anyone else hurt you?* He didn't ask. I wouldn't have told him the truth anyway. Maybe he knew that. We sat in silence. I shook my leg up and down. There was one more question I wanted to ask him: I wanted to know exactly who he'd tell if he learned someone had hurt me. I thought about the warnings my father had given me over the years. "It will kill your mother," he'd told me over and over again. "And you will be responsible for her death." Not wanting to be responsible for my mother jumping in front of a train, I decided it was best to keep that question to myself.

"Your mother told me you have bad dreams. Would you like to tell me about them?"

"Do you think having nightmares means I'm crazy?"

"Dreams aren't real, but nightmares can be really scary. Sometimes it helps you feel better if you talk about them."

I nodded. He was right. The dreams weren't real. Nobody could get in trouble if I talked about my dreams.

On the way home, traffic was heavier than it had been on the way to the office. My father had to focus on the road and not me. I felt like I could relax until we got home.

"What did you talk to Dr. W about?" my father asked when we stopped at a red light. He drove a manual-transmission car and kept one hand on the wheel and the other on the stick shift.

"Just stuff." I wrapped a strand of hair around my finger and gave it a tug.

"Speak English."

Without answering, I studied the light, willing it to change.

"I asked you a question."

"What I tell Dr. W is supposed to be confidential." I watched as the light turned green.

He didn't respond, but I could see the tension in his body from the way he sat up straighter and how his knuckles became white as he gripped the stick shift. I found his discomfort satisfying and had to fight the urge to smile.

When we stopped at the next red light, he looked over at me. "While you're keeping things confidential, remember who is in charge around here, little girl."

I stared straight ahead until the light changed again and he shifted the car back into first gear. A few minutes later, I saw the yellow McDonald's arches in the distance. I waited, and when we were a few feet away I put my hand on top of my father's.

such a pretty picture

"Daddy," I said, using my sweetest voice, "do you think we could bring McDonald's home for dinner? I'm really in the mood for a chocolate shake."

I began to see Dr. W every Thursday. After the first visit, my mother took me. She usually had Sarai with her, so instead of going upstairs, they'd drop me off in front of the building. "We'll run a few errands and be back here at five."

With time, the Thursday afternoon visits became familiar. Almost comforting. The blonde lady was always there waiting for her blonde daughter, who I had secretly nicknamed Julie. Whenever Julie came out, I studied her carefully. Checking out her clothes, her hairstyle, and her shoes. Most importantly, I made sure she was still wearing the chunky ID bracelet.

At home, in my spare time, I created an entire story revolving around Julie. I had replaced my pink diary with a black-and-white composition book. Although it wasn't pretty, the bigger lines and the margins made it easier to write. In my story, Julie's boyfriend was a high school sophomore named Sean. He had long brown hair and played guitar in a band after school. Like Ponyboy Curtis, Sean was sensitive and smart but poor, with grease under his fingernails and sneakers with holes. Julie's mother didn't like him. He wasn't good enough for her daughter, and she'd forced Julie to see Dr. W until she broke up with Sean. Each week that Julie showed up with the ID bracelet, love triumphed.

One day, after I'd been seeing Dr. W for about three months, the ID bracelet was missing, replaced by a thin gold watch. I immediately labeled the watch as a bribe. I checked for the ID bracelet the next week and the week after. Gone. The relationship was over, Julie's mother had won. My heart broke for Julie, and for me. That wasn't the way the story was supposed to end. I wanted a happy ending, although, truthfully, I wasn't sure what that meant. After a few weeks, Julie disappeared. A sad-looking boy of about eight or nine took her place. I felt sorry for him, but he wasn't interesting enough to write about.

By then, I'd begun to tell Dr. W more. I told him how I had trouble making friends, how I hated moving, and how being the new girl in school every year sucked. I even told him my parents fought about everything and nothing. He always listened carefully, and never treated me like a crazy twelve-year-old who needed to be fixed or locked away in an attic. I began to trust him as much as I'd ever trusted anyone. But no matter how much I trusted him, I kept my real secrets—the deals I made with my father, what my father did to me, and how I once even caused my mother to go blind—to myself.

chapter 20

After I started seeing Dr. W, my father touched me less—once a month at most. I wasn't sure if it was because he'd realized Dr. W wasn't going to let him lock me away or if, despite his arrogance, he'd started to worry that I might tell. Then again, maybe he'd just become too busy to bother with me. My father had finished his textbook, and had started a side business writing grants to help colleges get money. My mother told me that he'd become important. He also had a new friend, Nora, who worked with my father at the college. I'd never met her, but I'd overheard my parents fighting about her. Regardless of the reason, I felt grateful. For me, the less I saw of him, the better. If it weren't for my mother, I would have been happy if he'd disappeared altogether.

The summer between sixth and seventh grade, our family moved again, this time into our own home. Coral-colored with four bedrooms, a pool, and a backyard, this house was the prettiest one we'd ever lived in. On the day we moved in, my mother promised us it would be the last time. She'd never said that before. I felt a sense of permanence I hadn't experienced since we left Oyster Bay. For the first time, I even got a say in decorating my room. Although I had to keep the same furniture, my parents let me paint one wall shocking pink and put up a poster of James Taylor. Sarai got to decorate her room too, except she painted her wall lavender and picked Snoopy for her poster.

Andrea Leeb

About a week after we moved, my parents took us to an animal shelter and let us each pick out a cat. Mine was a kitten, an orange tabby with green eyes. I had wanted a female calico cat and had planned to name her Callie, but they didn't have any. It didn't matter. The second I set eyes on the tabby, he was mine. I called him Callie anyway. Sarai picked out a slightly older cat, a lilac point Siamese she named Farfel.

At Maitland Junior High School where I started seventh grade, the students matriculated from several elementary schools. Some took buses; others like me walked. For once, I wasn't the only new kid. That fall, everything felt better. Even my nightmares became less frequent. I began to think my parents had been right after all when they decided to send me to Dr. W.

The Saturday before Thanksgiving, I stood in front of my bedroom mirror, dressed in a pair of high-waisted bell-bottom jeans and a training bra I didn't need but insisted on wearing. My freshly washed hair was wrapped in a towel, and in each hand I held a sweater. One was a crewneck with pink and lavender stripes, the other a royal-blue V-neck.

I had plans to go to a rock concert in my school gym with Nancy and Kelly, two girls from my homeroom. The band wasn't famous, but they played at colleges in Gainesville and Tallahassee. I had never been to a concert or anything that resembled a school dance. I wanted to look perfect.

I had grown over the past year. At five feet tall and eighty-three pounds, no one mistook me for a ten-year-old anymore. At school, boys had begun to flirt with me, and I flirted back. I had a crush on one, a blond boy with brown eyes named Scott. On Friday at lunch, he'd asked me to meet him at the concert. I'd told Kelly that if he tried to kiss me, I'd let him. The blue sweater or the pink? I wanted another opinion, but my mother was at the

such a pretty picture

hairdresser and Sarai at a friend's house. My father was away too, on a business trip, and not due back until Sunday. I wouldn't have asked him anyway. I looked at my watch: a quarter to five. My mother had told me she'd be back by five thirty. I'd dry my hair and ask her when she got home.

I'd just finished drying when I heard the front door open and shut.

"Mom, I need your help." I ran into the hallway in my training bra and jeans.

"It's not Mom." My father stood in front of me with his suit bag in one hand and his briefcase in the other. "Are you the only one home?"

I covered my bra with my arms and nodded. He put his bags down and laughed.

"You don't need to act shy with me."

He took my hands in his. He smelled like booze and cigarettes. I noticed a spot of bright orange lipstick on his collar.

"You've become a beautiful woman." He let go of one of my hands and curled a lock of my hair around his fingers.

My throat closed and my skin felt itchy. I wanted to get away from him.

"Mom will be home soon," I said.

"Come closer." He drew me to him.

A cold shock ran through my body. I pulled away.

"Don't be coy." He reached for me again. Our bodies touched. Opening his lips, he brought his face closer to mine.

"No!" I screamed. "Leave me alone!" I pushed against his chest with my fists. "I don't want to do this."

He held my waist tightly.

Something inside of me snapped. I felt like I was in a tornado. Except this time the tornado wasn't in my dream or on the TV. This time the tornado was in me. "I hate you," I screamed and started to cry. Not tears but violent heaving sobs. I punched at him again, harder.

He put his hands up. "Calm down."

I heard the sound of the garage door opening. My father must have heard it too. Stepping away from me, he picked up his suit bag and briefcase.

"Go to your room and pull yourself together."

In my room, I threw myself on my bed. I had thought things were getting better. This time had not been the worst, but it terrified me. In the past, my father had touched me and I'd touched him, but he'd never tried to kiss me. *What if he did? What would come after?* I knew about sex, about intercourse. Fucking, the boys at school called it. Even before I knew what sex was, I'd been dreading the moment when my father would stick his penis inside of me. *Had the time finally come? Had he just been waiting for me to get old enough to do it?* I'd been honest when I told Dr. W that I wasn't like Anna. I poked and plucked to cause myself pain, but only because the pain made me feel better, not worse. I didn't want to kill myself. But if my father forced me to have sex with him—to fuck him—and if I let him, I didn't think I could go on. Whatever it was my father and I were doing had to end.

About fifteen minutes later, my mother knocked on my door. Letting herself in, she sat down on my bed.

My mother's freshly cut hair looked nice. She wore it gamine-short like the actress Mia Farrow. With her high cheekbones and fine features, she had the perfect face for it. My cheekbones were high too, but not defined like hers. I had my father's heavier features. My father might go on about how I reminded him of Sophia Loren, but I'd never be as beautiful as my mother.

"We need to talk," she said. "I can't understand why you always pick fights with your father."

such a pretty picture

"What did he tell you?" I wiped my wet face with the back of my hand.

"That he inadvertently said something to upset you. That you overreacted and threw a full-on tantrum."

He'd trapped me again. He knew I couldn't tell her the truth.

"I didn't throw a tantrum," I sobbed.

She pursed her lips and made a tsking sound. "You're completely hysterical." She looked me over. "Were you dressed like that when you were talking to your father?"

"I thought he was you," I said, still sobbing.

She shook her head. "You're too old to run around the house in a bra."

I put my hands over my face. *Stop*, I said to myself. I checked my watch. Kelly and her mother were picking me up in a half hour. "I have to finish getting ready."

"There's nothing to get ready for. I already called Kelly's mother and told her you were sick."

"What!" I jumped up. My mother knew how much I wanted to go to the concert. How excited I'd been when Kelly and Nancy asked me to come. I'd even told her about Scott, leaving out the planned kiss.

"You're a mess. We can't let you leave the house like this. God knows what you'll say."

I wanted to slap her. "Go away. I don't want to talk to you." I started to cry again.

"You've got to get hold of yourself." My mother stood up and walked out of my room, closing the door behind her.

I spent the rest of that evening, and the following day, in my room, crying and listening to James Taylor. I must've played the song "Fire and Rain" a hundred times. Surprisingly, my parents left me alone. Only Sarai came to my room. She brought me sandwiches and chocolate chip cookies to eat, Callie and Farfel to pet, and cold rags to press against my tear-swollen face.

chapter 21

Because of Thanksgiving, I didn't see Dr. W that Thursday. In the twelve days between the night of the missed concert and my next appointment, my father stayed away from me. Far away. He hardly spoke to me at all. I began to wonder if he had understood what I'd meant when I told him I was done. I thought about this possibility a lot. He had stopped before, but as soon as I felt secure, he began again. I hated it, but I had always let him, and I blamed myself for that. But now I wanted it to stop. Not just for days or weeks or even months, but forever. I wanted to be normal.

I decided that Dr. W was my only chance. I knew my parents met with him every month to talk about my progress. I hated it when they went to those meetings, but maybe there was a way to use them to help me. If I told Dr. W a little about the way my father treated me, he might mention it to my parents. And that might be enough to scare my father away for good. I knew I still needed to protect my mother, but I had to let my father know I was finally old enough and angry enough to talk, even if I'd never tell anyone the whole truth.

The day of the appointment, I told myself I had to be careful, to think about every word and not to bring anything up too quickly. At school, I could barely concentrate. All day, I imagined my meeting with Dr. W. Sitting in my classes, I silently rehearsed what I planned to tell him.

When I walked in his office, I plopped onto the couch.

such a pretty picture

Dr. W smiled at me. "How was your Thanksgiving?"

"My father calls me his little Sophia Loren." Forgetting the lines I'd prepared, I blurted out the words.

Dr. W shifted in his chair and picked up his notepad. "Can you tell me more about that?"

"Um, you know . . . she's beautiful." My left leg jiggled uncontrollably, and I put my hand on top of my knee to try to stop it.

"You seem nervous."

"I had a bad day at school." I sat facing him for a minute without talking. *How was I going to do this? Did I want to?*

"Tell me what your father says to you about Sophia Loren."

"He thinks she's sexy and beautiful."

"Did he say anything else?"

"Nothing else." I shook my head.

"Are you sure?"

I closed my eyes for a few seconds before answering. "He showed me a picture of her that he tore out of a magazine."

Dr. W's forehead furrowed and he frowned. It was the first time I'd seen any kind of expression on his face. "Do you know which magazine?"

I shrugged. I wondered why he'd asked that. "A regular magazine. Maybe my mother's *Vogue*. She was dressed in an evening gown."

His forehead softened, but his eyes scrunched as if he were trying to think about what to say next. "Has your father ever told you were sexy? Sexy like Sophia Loren?"

"Yes," I mumbled. I'd only wanted to create a vague suspicion. Had I gone too far or just far enough?

"Andrea, I have to ask you a question that might disturb you. I want you to tell me the truth."

I took a deep breath, wishing I'd never said anything. I wanted to change the subject, but I couldn't think of anything to say. My armpits itched; I had to clasp my hands together to stop from scratching.

"Has your father ever touched you?"

"Touched?" I saw myself standing in the hallway in my training bra as my father pulled me closer.

"Touched your breasts or your private parts."

I'd gone too far. My father would get out of it. He'd blame me. Then he'd lock me away and my mother would let him. I imagined sticking myself with a pin—felt the point piercing my skin. Once, twice, three, four times. The fantasy pain calmed me. "That would be gross." I made a gagging face. "Disgusting."

He studied me as if he were trying to see inside my brain. Did he believe me? I thought about my mother and my sister. If I got my father in trouble, their lives would be ruined too. *Why did I open my big mouth?*

"When he says I'm sexy, he means it as a compliment," I explained. "Like I'm pretty."

"I understand," Dr. W said.

I smiled, a strained smile, and my insides crumbled.

Although he didn't say so, I knew Dr. W would call my parents. When I got home, while the rest of the family were in the kitchen, I snuck into my parents' bedroom and took the phone off the hook. If I could delay the call long enough to see Dr. W again, I'd be able to straighten everything out. I'd tell him I lied to get my father in trouble because he grounded me. I'd look vindictive but it would be worth it. I took the phone off the hook the next afternoon too, but I was too late.

That evening, my mother, Sarai, and I stood in the kitchen making spaghetti and meatballs for dinner.

"Sarai," my mother said after we'd finished rolling the last meatball, "the cats are crying. Go make sure they aren't in Daddy's office."

"I don't hear anything," Sarai said.

such a pretty picture

"Just check for me, and make sure you look in the bedrooms and under the beds. Check the closets too."

As soon as Sarai left, my mother turned to me. "Dr. W called me at work today."

"He did?" Using a knife, I spread garlic butter inside a loaf of French bread.

"He wants us to come in."

"Farfel, Callie," I heard Sarai calling. I smeared another dollop of butter on the loaf.

"Enough with the bread. Pay attention to me."

Still holding the knife, I turned to face her.

"He wants to meet with us tomorrow at nine."

"On a Saturday?" I ran my fingers on the blade of the knife, wishing it were sharper. I wondered what it would be like to cut my skin with it. Something I had never thought about before.

"He sounded concerned. Is there anything I need to know?"

I pressed the dull blade of the knife against my palm. "I don't think so. Isn't it time for your regular meeting with him?" I gazed out our kitchen window into the backyard. Both cats sat together on a chaise lounge, their faces turned to the sky as if they were trying to catch the last rays of the late afternoon sun.

"If there is something I should know, tell me. I want to be prepared."

"I already said there's nothing." I pointed to the chaise lounge. "Is it okay if I tell Sarai we found the cats?" I put the knife down.

That night, I couldn't sleep. I tried to read, but the chatter in my head destroyed my concentration. I lay in my bed stroking Callie's fur and listening to him purr as I dissected my conversation with Dr. W. I imagined what he would say to my parents and how they would react. The images of my mother's distraught face and the rage in my father's eyes were too much for me. *Think about something else*, I told myself, but I couldn't. Instead, I got out of bed. Opening the second drawer of my dresser, I took out a red pincushion I kept hidden under my T-shirts.

I had stopped pricking for a month when we first moved to the coral-colored house. When I began again, I restarted my count at zero and promised myself I would never go over twenty pricks. Since the night of the concert, I was already back up to a hundred. Fifty on one thigh, fifty on the other. It hurt, but the sting of each prick released a tiny red bubble of internal pain. And it was safer than using a knife.

"No more than one hundred and ten," I said out loud as I stuck the pin into the top of my right thigh.

When I woke, my parents were already gone. Sarai was still sleeping and I didn't wake her. I wanted to be alone. Our backyard had several orange trees. Sarai and I were responsible for fishing fallen leaves and oranges out of the pool. When we moved in, my father had bought us each a net so we could do it together. A job neither of us liked, but that morning it was a good distraction.

After I'd finished, I sat with my legs dangling in the cool water. The air smelled like chlorine and orange blossoms. Behind me, I heard a chirping sound. Two black and yellow birds were gathering twigs to make themselves a nest in one of the orange trees. Callie was a bird charmer. Birds froze in mid-flight when he called them. If they built their nest in our yard, they wouldn't last a day. I stood up and clapped my hands.

"I'm sorry," I said as they flew away. "But this is not a safe place."

I sat back down. I didn't want to be inside when my parents came home. From my poolside perch, I'd be able to see them walk into the kitchen before they saw me.

They came home about fifteen minutes later. Watching them through the window, my stomach churned as I thought about the

such a pretty picture

inevitable conversation. My father had his back toward me, but my mother faced the backyard. Seeing me, she waved. She must have told my father, because a few seconds later he came outside.

The sliding doors opened from our dining room to a tile patio with a round table and four chairs. My father sat down at the table.

"The pool looks clean. Good job."

"Thanks." I ran my fingers over the pinpricks on my upper thighs. They were almost invisible, but if I pressed on them I could make myself hurt.

"Too bad the forecast calls for rain later today."

I rolled my eyes. The pool always got filled with leaves when it rained. I squinted at the sky. Not a single cloud in sight, but in Florida you could only depend on the weather for a moment.

"I need to talk to you," my father said.

Grudgingly, I walked to the table and then slumped into the seat across from him. I could see my mother watching us from the kitchen. I wondered why she didn't come outside too. "Dr. W told us that you are a very confused little girl."

My hands were on my lap. I clenched them and dug my nails into my palms. My father called me a little girl only when he wanted to make me feel bad about myself.

"He said you have an abnormal obsession with me. He said most little girls fall in love with their father, but with you it's extreme. A sickness. It's called an Oedipal complex."

I couldn't tell if he was lying. "Dr. W said I was sick?" I pressed my fingers against the pinpricks on my thighs.

"You and I need to spend less time together, until you get your fantasies under control."

"What does that mean?" I asked. "The 'getting the fantasies under control' part?" My father's voice sounded calm, but I saw the fury in his eyes.

"I think you're smart enough to know what it means."

As soon as we came inside, my father locked himself in his office. By then, Sarai had gotten up. I wanted to find a way to get my mother alone without making a big deal of it. I wanted to ask her about Dr. W. Had he really called me sick? Had he blamed me and not my father? I told myself I shouldn't care who got blamed so long as my father stayed away from me, but I couldn't help feeling like I'd been betrayed.

After lunch it started to rain, and my mother offered to take Sarai and me to the skating rink for the afternoon. We both loved to roller-skate. We had the whole getup: polished white skates with pink and blue pom-poms on the laces, headbands and short pleated skirts—mine black and Sarai's white. My mother rarely came inside the rink with us. Sometimes she went home, but most of the time she sat in her car and graded papers or worked on her lesson plans. I think she liked the time away from everyone. Normally, I'd be thrilled to spend an entire afternoon at the roller rink, but that day it meant there would be no time to get my mother alone.

When we got home, I went upstairs to change before dinner. Walking into my room, I saw a book on my bed, *The Scarlet Letter*. My father must have left it for me. I didn't know what the book was about, but I knew if he'd left it, there had to be a reason. Unsure if I wanted to know what my father wanted me to learn, I put it on my shelf.

That night, a few minutes after I turned off my light, my mother knocked on my door.

"Can I come in?" she asked, then came in and flipped on the light before I could respond. "Did you have fun skating?" She sat on the end of my bed.

"I always have fun skating." I sat up into a crossed-legged position. I knew my mother was not there to ask me about skating. "Are you going to tell me what Dr. W said?"

such a pretty picture

"Your father already talked to you."

"I want to hear it from you, not him."

"Actually, I came in here to talk to you about your father." My body stiffened and my heart thrummed inside my chest. I didn't know what to expect.

"You know your father doesn't get along with his mother."

I nodded. We saw my father's family only occasionally and weren't as close to them as my mother's family. His father had died after our second summer in Florida, but only my parents went to the funeral, and they didn't stay to sit shiva. I had always heard that he and my grandmother favored my father's much younger brother.

As we sat on my bed, my mother told me about my father's childhood. How his mother didn't hug him, how she hit him and never bought him new clothes or toys. How she called him stupid and worthless. Listening to my mother talk, I wondered if she remembered what she'd done to me when I was small: the way she'd hit me and how horrible she'd made me feel.

"His mother used to put a dog collar around his neck," my mother said.

"What did you say?" I thought I'd misheard her.

"She put a collar on him and chained him to a tree in back of their apartment building. She did it until he was three or four. She'd leave him chained from morning to night. She even fed him his meals out there. He had to pee against the tree like a dog."

"Didn't the neighbors call the police?"

"People didn't get involved back then."

I wondered if the story was true, then I thought about the pictures I'd seen of my father as a child. A chubby little boy with curly black hair and knickers. The idea of that cute little boy—my father—chained to a tree broke my heart. Even if the story was only partially true, it made me feel bad about how much I hated him. *How could I hate someone who had been so hurt himself? How could I blame him for what he did to me?*

Andrea Leeb

"We need to be kind to him. Sometimes he doesn't think about what he's doing, but we must forgive him. He's a damaged man, but he needs us. All of us."

I started to cry and for once my mother didn't try to stop me. She held me and rocked me in her arms. I wept for at least an hour. I didn't know if my tears were for him or for me or for both of us. It didn't matter.

I never saw Dr. W again. I don't know exactly what he said to my parents or what, if anything, he did afterward. At first, I thought he might tell someone else, report it. But when nothing happened, I decided that he either didn't believe me or didn't think I was worth his time.

Dr. W didn't come to my rescue but, as it turned out, my plan had succeeded. I read *The Scarlet Letter* a few weeks later and saw it as my final warning. If anyone ever found out about what had happened between my father and me, I'd end up like Hester: marked, alone and unbelieved, a blood-red letter permanently sewn onto my chest. When I finished the book, I made myself a promise never to tell anyone. No matter what, I would keep what had happened between my father and me secret.

chapter 22

My father lost his job a few months after I stopped seeing Dr. W. A late-spring long-weekend jaunt with some publishing buddies turned into a ten-day vacation. He missed classes and meetings and forgot to call home. My mother, alone with my sister and me, fumed. By midsummer, he'd found another job: a better one, as an associate dean at another community college in New Jersey. My mother forgave and forgot. Old enough to understand, I bore witness but said nothing.

We left the coral-colored house in July. Sarai, my mother, and I, along with our two cats, flew up north, sparing us all another family road trip. My parents paid one of my father's students to drive my mother's Oldsmobile, and my father drove his car. Supposedly, he drove alone, but later I'd learn he'd been accompanied by Nora, his mysterious coworker who, unbeknownst to my mother, had gotten a job at the same college. My father and Nora would be lovers for the next twenty years.

On a sweltering day in mid-August, my family, the two cats included, sat in gridlocked traffic on the small iron bridge connecting Lambertville, New Jersey, to New Hope, Pennsylvania. Below us, the Delaware River sparkled in the sunlight. Around us, impatient drivers honked their horns.

Andrea Leeb

New Hope, the town where my parents had decided we would live, was thirty minutes from my father's new college, and twenty in the opposite direction from the elementary school where my mother would be teaching. "You're going to love it," my mother had told us a few days before. "Lots of trees, craft and antique stores, and a famous playhouse. The perfect place to grow up." Listening to her, I rolled my eyes. At almost thirteen and a half, I already felt grown up, and I'd long stopped believing in perfect places.

That day as I sat in the back seat sweating, listening to my father curse and my mother complain, New Hope didn't seem so perfect. An imperfection compounded by the news that, instead of a house, my parents had bought a plot of land. It would be months before the house was built. Until then, we were going to live in a motel.

The wooden sign at the entrance said Bucks County Motel. We parked in front of a two-story house with a bay window. Behind it was a one-story, L-shaped cement building. Both were painted white, not a clean white, but a gray-white. It reminded me of dirty city snow. One of the shutters had fallen off the bay window of the house. It lay broken in pieces on the gravel driveway.

A short woman with curlers came outside and waved at us. The place looked so bedraggled, I wondered if she'd been expecting us or if she was just glad that someone, anyone, might be willing to check in. My parents got out of the car, leaving us inside.

"This place looks gross," I said to Sarai.

"Do you think we are really going to live here?"

"Maybe it's just for one night and we'll go to the permanent motel tomorrow," I said, hoping without hope. "Either way, better not say a word."

A few minutes later, my father opened the door to rooms 104 and 105.

such a pretty picture

"Home," he said, and motioned for the three of us to go inside. The place smelled moldy and dank. My parents had a "suite" with a small living room and a kitchen area with a mini refrigerator, a coffee maker, and a hot plate. An old air-conditioning unit under the window blew air that felt more moist than cold. The furniture looked exhausted, and the olive-colored shag carpeting, filthy. A door from the living room led to a bedroom with a king-sized bed and a dresser. I wondered how my mother, a woman who vacuumed at least four times a week and spent every Sunday morning scrubbing the base molding of whatever house or apartment we lived in, had agreed to this pigsty.

The room Sarai and I were to share had two double beds and was as run-down as the suite. As soon as we put down our bags, my mother stripped all of the beds and inspected each mattress, lifting them and looking underneath. "For bugs or spiders," she said. Then she instructed Sarai and me to put the bedspreads into the green plastic garbage bags she'd brought with her. "Double-bag them and stick them in the back of the closet. And when you're finished, run over to the manager's office and tell her we need fresh sheets. After tonight, we'll wash them ourselves."

We spent the rest of the day scrubbing the inside of the dressers and the bathrooms with Lysol (another item my mother brought with her) and unpacking our clothing. By the time we finished, our cats had killed three mice.

That evening, we had an early dinner of pizza on a picnic table a few feet from our room. "This isn't so bad," my mother said.

Taking in the overgrown grass and the beer cans scattered in the gravel parking lot, I bit my tongue.

My parents said goodnight right after dinner, leaving us alone in our room. As Sarai and I lay on our beds watching a *Partridge Family* rerun, I heard the sound of doors slamming and men's voices. It wasn't yet completely dark. Looking out the window, I saw a row of big trucks parked at the back of the lot. A group of men, smoking cigarettes and drinking beer out of cans, sat around the picnic table where we'd had our dinner.

I walked to the door, yanked at the chain, and then twisted the handle to make sure it was locked. "Remember to keep the chain on the door," I said to Sarai.

There was a Magic Fingers box mounted on the wall above each of our beds. Our mother had left a small stack of quarters for each of us on our nightstands. Sarai took one and put it into the box.

"This is fun," she giggled as her bed began to shake and hum. "Come over."

I lay down next to her. When the shaking stopped, she put another quarter in. I didn't like the movement, but I stayed put. The room had a strange damp feeling, and Sarai's body felt warm and safe next to mine.

Ignoring the humming bed, our cats lay cuddled together in front of the closet. I wondered how many more mice they'd kill before morning.

One of the men in the parking lot laughed loudly.

I gave Sarai a poke. "If you're ever alone in here, don't let anyone come into our room except me or Mommy."

"What about Daddy?"

"Daddy?" I glanced at the door connecting our room to our parents' suite. Earlier, my mother forbade me from locking the dead bolt. "What if there's a fire?" she said, like she always did. As if a fire were the worst thing we had to worry about.

"Can Daddy come in?"

My body felt hot and then cold. I had been warning her about the truckers outside and not my father. I had long ago decided that, although he hit and yelled at Sarai, he had never touched her in the way he touched me. It wasn't just a feeling. Over the years, I'd watched my sister's room carefully. After he stopped touching me, I checked her bed for semen stains when no one was looking.

such a pretty picture

I'd never seen any evidence. On top of that, Sarai was my mother's favorite, her baby. I had absolute faith that she would protect Sarai from that one thing. I'd convinced myself that, like a twist on the story of Demeter and Persephone, my mother had surrendered one daughter to Hades in exchange for protecting the other.

"Has Daddy come into your room when you are alone?"

"Daddy doesn't like me the same way he likes you."

I choked. I wanted to ask her what she meant by that, but I was too afraid of her answer.

"Are you okay?" she asked.

"I thought I swallowed a bug." I feigned a gag.

"That's gross," she giggled, and pretended to stick a finger in her throat.

Taking a quarter off the nightstand, I slipped it into the box. "Let's declare this a girls-only room. No boys allowed." I wrapped my arms around her as the bed began to shake.

chapter 23

On a Tuesday afternoon in early December, I sat in a booth at the Golden Pump diner with my friend Katherine. School had let out for the day and we were eating French fries soaked in ketchup and drinking Cokes before we each made our way home.

"Diane's having a party this weekend." Katherine lit a cigarette. "Boys and girls, there'll be kids from other schools. You should come."

"I don't know Diane very well."

"I'm inviting you. Diane will be cool with it." Katherine took another hit off the cigarette and handed it to me. She watched me take a puff. "I need to teach you how to smoke."

Pretty, with auburn hair and green eyes, Katherine was the coolest girl in our class. I couldn't believe a girl like her had picked me to be her friend. After a month, I'd worked up the courage to ask her why. "You're smart and you're pretty," she explained, "but nowhere near as smart or as pretty as I am." I took it as praise.

Shortly after arriving at the party, I learned that Diane's mother wasn't home. "She's on a date," Diane told me. "She won't be back until after midnight." I didn't say anything, but I was surprised her mother would let a houseful of teenagers have a party without an adult around. The butterflies I'd felt all day morphed into

such a pretty picture

crows. As Diane showed me where to put my coat, they flapped frantically in my stomach.

"The party's in the basement." She pointed to an open door in the hallway.

We sat in a circle on the cement floor, passing a joint and a bottle of Boone's Farm Strawberry Hill wine. It was the first time I was with kids my age drinking and smoking pot. A flashing disco ball hanging from the ceiling cast slivers of glittery light in the dark basement. The only other light came from a single bulb at the top of the stairs. I'd purposely left my glasses upstairs in my coat. I blinked and tried to adjust my already blurry eyes to the dark. "Stairway to Heaven" blasted from a portable stereo. I knew all the words, and hearing it made me feel like I belonged. The air smelled smoky and fragrant, a strange combination of incense, pot, and patchouli. I sat cross-legged between Katherine and another girl named Barb.

"I like your top," Katherine whispered, and I laughed. Even though it was winter, we'd both decided to wear tube tops. Katherine had two. She'd lent me one a few days before the party.

"I had to put a sweater over it to get out of the house," I said.

Katherine laughed. "Me too." Her auburn hair shimmered under the silver disco ball.

I watched Katherine take the joint. She put it to her lips and inhaled. Then, with an almost imperceptible cough, she exhaled.

"Inhale and hold it," she whispered in my ear as she handed me the joint. I'd confessed to her earlier on the telephone that I'd never smoked pot.

My hands shook as I put the joint up to my lips. Grateful for the dark, I inhaled a tiny bit of smoke. I felt Katherine's eyes on me, so I inhaled again, deeper this time. As I swallowed the smoke, the back of my throat burned. I tried not to cough but couldn't help myself. Once I started, I couldn't stop. Embarrassed and still coughing, I passed the joint to Barb.

Andrea Leeb

"This will help." Katherine passed me a bottle of wine. She leaned into her boyfriend, Peter, who sat on the other side of her.

I took a sip. It tasted sweet, like juice mixed with strawberry syrup. Another first. I took another sip and passed the bottle. A cute boy named Daniel sat across the circle from me, talking to one of the other girls. Wiry with light brown curly hair, dimples, and an upturned nose, he was a ninth grader in one of the nearby private schools. I had heard he played guitar in a real band—not just a school band. We'd met once before and talked about records and bands. My eyes burned from the smoke and the strain of trying to see without my glasses. Everyone seemed to be talking to someone. The feeling of belonging I'd had when I walked in faded. Like always, I was an outsider. As if the party was happening around me, but I wasn't there.

The bottle came around again. I took one sip and then another, not a sip but a gulp. It calmed me. The negative voice in my head dulled.

"Let's play spin the bottle," I heard one of the boys say.

Some girls shook their heads no. They drifted away, forming another circle at the other side of the room, the good girl circle. All of the boys stayed. I glanced at Katherine, looking for my cue. She sat holding hands with Peter. I wanted to join the good girls. I'd been kissed before, but only by a boy I liked, not some random boy.

A boy named Greg spun first. He went to the same private school as Daniel, and I'd heard they were best friends. He was a doughy boy with acne. *Please don't let it be me*, I prayed silently. When the bottle pointed at Diane, she groaned. "No way. I'm out." She giggled and joined the girls in the other circle.

Peter went next, but instead of spinning, he just started kissing Katherine.

"It's your turn," Greg shouted to me. I cringed at the thought of kissing him.

such a pretty picture

Tentatively, I touched the bottle and deliberately pointed it in Daniel's direction. I couldn't believe I had it in me to be that bold.

"No fair," Greg protested. "She rigged it."

Daniel stood up and reached for my hand. Elated, I prepared myself for a kiss, but he led me away from the circle to the other side of the basement. When he kissed me, I felt like my lips were on fire.

"I don't want to play that stupid game." He pointed to a mattress a few inches away. "Let's go over there."

My legs shook and I stumbled as I followed him. I felt everyone's eyes on us. Lying down on the mattress, he pulled me next to him. He kissed me again, this time with his tongue. My whole body flushed. Giddy with excitement, I let him slip his hands under my top.

I don't remember how long it was before Greg lay down next to us. Startled, I opened my eyes and sat up.

"Stop." I pushed Daniel away.

"What's wrong?" Daniel sat up and nuzzled my neck.

"Not 'til he leaves," I said, loud enough for Greg to hear.

"But I haven't had my turn yet." Greg rubbed my leg. I pushed his fingers away.

"It's okay," Daniel said, and kissed me.

They both rolled on top of me at once and yanked my tube top down. Four hands clawed at my breasts. Blending together as if they were one giant boy, I could no longer tell them apart. I wanted to leave, but I was frozen. Earlier that night when I'd dressed, I'd been pleased with my flat stomach and the way my hips poked out. I liked the way the top showed off my budding breasts. Arriving at the house, I'd felt pretty, and for once I was almost happy being me.

"Help me," one of them whispered as he fumbled with the buttons on my hip-huggers.

I refused. I lay stiffly, with my hands at my side, staring at the silver ball dangling from the ceiling. I watched it spin as the two

Andrea Leeb

boys slid their hands under my panties, their ragged fingernails ripping deep inside of me.

After it was over, I walked to where the other girls stood. They eyeballed me with an expression of disgust and pity. I realized right then that any other girl would have stopped them. Diane, Barb, or Katherine would have walked away. But I had no boundaries, no understanding of how to stop it once it began. Although my father had not touched me for over a year, he had trained me well. When the boys touched me, the only thing I knew how to do was to lie still and wait for it to be over.

chapter 24

My school was small enough for almost everyone to know what had happened. And to make it worse, there were rumors. The week after the party, while using the bathroom, I overheard two older girls gossiping about how I'd fucked three boys. "I heard she gives blow jobs too," one said to the other. They must've been smoking, because the smell of cigarette smoke drifted over the stall. My face burning, I sat on the toilet, pants around my ankles, until the bell rang and the bathroom door slammed shut.

Even some of the teachers seemed to know. My history teacher had a son in ninth grade; she lectured me about wearing my sweaters too tight and my jeans too low. "You distract the boys," she said. Alone, I cried, but by then I knew how to ignore things in public. I'd had a lifetime of practice. At first, all the girls from the party refused to talk to me. But after a couple weeks, Katherine decided, despite or maybe because of my bad reputation, that we should stay friends, which meant the rest of the kids in my grade had to act like they liked me even if they didn't. I forced myself to try to fit in. I joined drama club and got a part in the spring school play—not a starring role, but a good part with a long monologue.

In April, a few weeks after my fourteenth birthday, my family moved out of the motel and into our new house. By the time school ended, the gossip had died down. I knew from my other schools that kids' memories faded. I told myself that when school started again in September, my mistake at the party would be long forgotten.

"I heard you worked here." Chad leaned over the glass counter filled with chocolates. I stood on the other side, dressed in my white uniform and blue-and-white checkered apron. I'd been working full-time at the candy store since school let out, selling fudge and fancy chocolates to tourists from New York City, Philadelphia, or the New Jersey suburbs. They came to New Hope for the stores, the bars, and the Bucks County Playhouse. I used the money I made to buy albums and clothes. I liked the idea of being independent from my parents.

"You really heard that?" Chad didn't go to our school but was friends with a couple of the juniors. I vaguely knew who he was, having seen him from time to time at basketball games and hanging out in the parking lot. But we'd never talked, and I wondered why he would have heard or cared where I worked. I studied him, tall and skinny with a sharp nose and long brown hair. Not a boy I'd ever thought of as cute.

"I have a sweet tooth and come here sometimes, but you're never here. I always get waited on by Mrs. Claus."

I laughed. Abby, the store manager, with her white bun and plump red cheeks, did look like Mrs. Claus.

"Hey, don't you wear glasses?"

I blushed, embarrassed he'd noticed. "I got contacts this summer." I felt Abby's eyes on me. She had run the candy store for years and took it seriously. Visitors were strictly prohibited during work hours. "I need to take your order." I tilted my head in Abby's direction.

He pointed to the tray of fudge. "I'll take two squares."

I grabbed the fudge and weighed it. "Anything else?"

such a pretty picture

"You want to go to a party in Washington Crossing later?"

He caught me off guard. "I don't know anybody from Washington Crossing," I said.

Although only a few miles down the river from New Hope, Washington Crossing was in a different school district. To me that was a different world.

"There'll be other people from your school there, and you know me."

While I rang up his fudge and counted his change, I considered it. Since that first party, I'd grown more cautious. I didn't want to make my reputation any worse. I glanced at Chad. Until that day, we'd never said a word to each other. I didn't know him; I didn't even really know his friends. Still, except for the one at Diane's, I liked parties and I liked the attention from boys, especially older boys. That day, my parents and Sarai were in New York visiting Nanny. As long as I made it home by eleven, they wouldn't even know I'd gone out. What was the worst that could happen?

In the bathroom at the back of the store, I took off my white shoes, apron, and uniform, and changed into cutoff shorts, a yellow T-shirt, and my blue suede clogs. I lived about two miles from town, and usually walked home from work. I always changed first; I wouldn't be caught dead in my uniform in public. As I put my work clothes into my locker, I brought a strand of hair up to my nose. It smelled like chocolate. I wished I could go home, wash it, and change into something prettier, but Chad had insisted he needed to pick me up at the store right after work. "The party will be in full swing by the time we get there."

He picked me up a little after five thirty. I squinted in the late afternoon sun while we drove. We both had our windows open, and the warm, humid air massaged my face. Framed on one side by the Delaware River and on the other by trees and old stone houses, the road twisted and turned with the flow of the river.

"Do you like the Stones?" Chad slipped a cassette into the tape deck without waiting for me to answer.

When we got to Washington Crossing, we made a right onto another road.

"How far?" I asked. I had expected the party to be in town.

"Not much farther."

We drove for another twenty minutes. The landscape around us became more rural with every mile. I checked my watch three times.

"Is this still Washington Crossing?"

"Just outside of it."

A knot formed in my stomach. Nobody I knew would drive this far. "I thought the party was closer."

"Chill, baby, we'll be there soon." Chad changed the cassette deck to *Aqualung*—not one of my favorite albums. The title song about an old man eyeing schoolgirls creeped me out. I checked my watch again.

It was a quarter after six by the time we turned onto a gravel driveway and parked in front of a blue clapboard house surrounded by woods. I expected to see cars, but the driveway and the lawn in front of the house were empty.

"Are you sure this is the right place?"

"We're early," Chad said. He got out of the car, motioning me to follow.

"You said it started at five." I stood on the empty lawn, listening in vain for the sound of a party—the high-pitch buzz of teenage voices or the pulsing rhythm of rock and roll music. But the only sound I heard was my heart pounding.

"There's a cool old ruin in the woods." He started to walk behind the house, then turned and waited for me. "I bet everyone's already back there," he said, his eyes focused on the ground.

I followed him onto a path leading into the woods. After a few feet, the ground became uneven and rocky. Hard to navigate

such a pretty picture

in clogs, I kept my eyes down to avoid tripping. Branches from stray bushes scratched my bare legs. In long pants and desert boots, Chad walked several feet in front of me. If I turned around now, I'd probably be able to hitch a ride home before dark.

After another five minutes or so, we came to a clearing in the woods.

"Over there." Chad pointed to the ruins of what had once been an old stone house. Only the foundation and two stone walls remained.

Two boys sat against a crumbling stone wall with a case of Rolling Rock in front of them. It seemed like a lot of beer for four people, so maybe there would be a party after all.

"Finally," one boy said as we walked closer. He had blond shoulder-length hair and bright blue eyes. He was cute, but something about him made me nervous. He smiled at me and patted the ground next to him. The remnants of the fudge I'd snacked on earlier rose into my throat.

"Wanna beer?" the other boy said. Dark-haired and small, he seemed younger than the other two. Without waiting for an answer, he handed me a bottle.

I sat down and slipped my clogs off. I wondered if it'd be easier to run through the woods barefoot. I took a fake sip of beer. The boys were sweating, but my arms and legs were covered in goose bumps. I prayed for other girls to show up.

"I should get going," I said after the boys all finished their second beer.

"You can't let that beer go to waste," the blue-eyed boy said.

Ignoring him, I stood up. "Seems like the party is off." I tried to make eye contact with Chad. "You can stay, I'll hitch a ride home."

The blue-eyed boy stood up and faced me. He was close to my father's height. At least six three, he dwarfed my five-foot-two-inch, ninety-pound body.

"Party's just beginning, sweetheart." He pulled me against him. "Don't touch me." I pushed him away, but he grabbed my shoulder. "Chad, help me. Please help me."

Chad didn't budge. The blue-eyed boy laughed and I began to scream. I screamed so loud, I thought my vocal cords were going to split. It was pointless; no one but the three boys could hear me.

The blue-eyed boy put his hand over my mouth. I felt the calluses on his hands against my face. "What the fuck, Chad. I thought you said she was easy."

"I heard she fucked the whole soccer team," Chad said.

The blue-eyed boy still had his hand over my mouth. I bit him, hard enough to break his skin. Hard enough to taste his sour blood.

"You fucking bitch." He clamped down tighter. I couldn't breathe. My legs shook, and I dug my bare feet into the dirt to keep my balance. He threw me to the ground and climbed on top of me. He smelled like gasoline and beer. Sharp pebbles pierced the back of my legs. I pushed against him and kicked at him, but I missed his groin.

"Grab her," he said to the other two.

The sky turned a pinkish-blue. A mosquito hummed in my ear. The small boy held my arms. Chad grabbed my legs.

The blue-eyed boy yanked down my shorts and panties. "Spread her legs," he instructed Chad.

"I have to get her shorts off," Chad croaked. Releasing one leg and then the other, he deflected my kicks as he pulled off my shorts and panties. Then he stretched my right leg out so wide I thought my hip would pop out of its socket.

"You're hurting me!" I gasped.

I stopped fighting them, but when the blue-eyed boy tried to enter me, my body seized up. After years of submitting to my father's touch, it refused to surrender. Every part of me became as hard as a board. He pushed into me again and again, but he could

such a pretty picture

not enter. Was it me or him? I didn't know, but I did know that the harder he tried, the angrier he got. He slapped me twice, and then he got on his knees and pushed himself into my mouth.

"If you bite me again, we will kill you," he said.

By the time the other two took their turns, my body had completely deflated, but neither of them tried to enter me. One at a time, they stood above me, frantically stroking themselves, almost as if they had forgotten I was there. Afraid they might try to kill me, I forced myself to keep my eyes open while they came on my face and my chest.

When they were finished, all three boys stared at me while I grabbed my shorts and struggled to pull them up.

"If you tell anyone what happened we'll throw you in the river," the blue-eyed one said. "Not that anyone will believe you. Everyone knows you are a slut. Why do you think Chad brought you here?" He laughed, and the others laughed with him. Hard, brittle laughter.

I ran barefoot through the woods, holding a clog in each hand. Pebbles dug into the soles of my feet. I stubbed my toes against rocks and branches. I'd almost reached the house when I heard the sound of footsteps and breaking branches behind me.

"Slow down," Chad yelled. "I'll take you home."

Was he joking? Or was it a trick? Were the other two with him? Still running, I glanced over my shoulder. He was alone.

"It's getting dark. You're too young to hitchhike. It's dangerous."

I stopped and watched him walking toward me under the violet sky. It seemed so surreal, I felt like laughing and crying at the same time. Somewhere in the woods an owl hooted.

Afraid the blue-eyed one would come after me, I got into Chad's car. As we drove, he changed the cassette again. This time, Pink Floyd, *The Dark Side of the Moon*. When we got close to my house, I told him to drop me at the bottom of a steep hill. My street was halfway up the hill, but I didn't want him to know exactly where I lived.

Andrea Leeb

"Remember," he said before I got out of the car, "no one will believe you."

I stood in front of a dark house that wasn't mine and watched him pull away. Above me, stars glittered in the black, moonless sky. There were no streetlamps on the hill. Clusters of fireflies flickered in the fields between the houses. I sprinted up the road. The clatter of my wooden clogs hitting the pavement broke the silence.

My parents and sister wouldn't be back for hours. I ran up the stairs into the bathroom, and locked the door behind me. Stripping off my soiled clothing, I stepped into the shower. Then I turned the hot water up high, letting the blistering pellets burn my skin.

Once clean, I picked up my clothes. They smelled like sweat and semen. Just touching them made me gag. My mother kept a pair of scissors in the bathroom linen closet, big silver ones with black handles. I started with the T-shirt. The scissors slid easily through the thin cotton. The shorts were harder. Made from old Levi's jeans, the thick fabric resisted my cuts. Holding them, I hesitated. They'd been my favorite pair, but they were ruined for me forever. They had to be destroyed.

After I finished, I held the scissors in my hand and studied myself in the mirror. An ache rose from deep in my chest. An unrelenting pain. I needed to do something to make it go away.

I made the cut slowly. I did it on my lower stomach, a place where no one else would see. Just enough to bleed—to feel the comforting sting as beads of blood bubbled to the surface of my skin. I thought about making a second cut, but I realized I didn't need to. I was in control.

chapter 25

I never saw Chad or the other boys from the woods again. The blue-eyed one and the smaller one lived in a different town, so I knew it would be unlikely. More afraid of seeing Chad, I quit my job at the candy store just in case. I kept an eye out for him around town, but he seemed to have vanished. Maybe he was afraid of me too.

With time, I'd come to realize that my father had groomed me not only for himself but for the boys at the party, the boys in the woods, and all of the other boys and men that followed. As a child, I thought my father owned me. I had no agency over my body and no awareness of boundaries. My father had taught me to live in fear. A lesson I didn't remember the day I naively followed Chad into the woods, but one that I would not forget again.

Although I didn't see the boys from the woods, I spent most of ninth grade hiding my face behind a curtain of thick hair. I stopped wearing my contact lenses and reverted to oversized wire-frame glasses. I wanted to disappear. By early spring, it became impossible. I was fifteen, and my body had changed without my permission. My flat breasts blossomed and by the end of the school year, I wore a full C cup. The parts of me that were once sharp, bony angles morphed into soft curves.

Andrea Leeb

In May, I got a job at a jewelry store in town, selling gold-plated earrings and fake turquoise bracelets. My first day of work was the Saturday of Memorial Day weekend. It was a cold and rainy day but, excited for my new job and the imminent arrival of summer, I wore a blue Indian print halter dress, tan wedge sandals, and a pair of small silver hoops. After almost a year of hiding, I wanted to shine.

I worked with another girl named Terri. Two years older than me, she went to an all-girls Catholic school. I met her for the first time when I'd applied for the job. That rainy Saturday morning, we didn't have a single customer. Terri and I passed the time reading old copies of *Tiger Beat* and *Seventeen*. Right around noon, Terri's boyfriend and another boy stopped in for a visit. A welcome distraction.

"I'm going to take a break in the back room," Terri said.

I wondered if this kind of "break" was allowed but didn't say anything. As Terri and her boyfriend shut the door behind them, the other boy leaned against a small bench in front of the window.

"I'm Brian." He grinned at me.

Tallish, skinny, with shoulder-length sandy hair, Brian wore bell-bottom jeans, platforms, and a paisley polyester shirt. I preferred hippie boys, the kind who dressed in faded Levi 501s, flannel shirts, and hiking boots, but Brian seemed nice enough. And, I learned, Brian lived in Lambertville. Although Lambertville was only a five-minute walk across the bridge, Lambertville and New Hope kids rarely mixed. It felt good to talk to a boy who didn't know anything about me.

We stood with the counter between us while Brian told me about himself. He'd lived in Lambertville his whole life. His father

such a pretty picture

worked at the paper factory on the river. About to finish his junior year of high school, Brian had no plans for college.

"I'm thinking about the Army," he said.

"I'm against the war. I went to the big march in Washington right after Nixon got reelected."

"The war's almost over. I just want to go to Germany or England, anywhere that's not here."

"As soon as I graduate, I'm out of here too." I didn't mention that I'd already started making lists of out-of-state colleges. I didn't want to brag.

I heard Terri giggling in the back room.

Brian smirked. "They'll be in there for a while." He sat down on the bench and patted the space next to him. "You may as well take a seat. Nobody's coming into town in this weather."

I hesitated.

He patted the bench again. "I promise I won't bite."

I sat down next to him, careful our bodies didn't touch. Terri and her boyfriend were only twenty feet away; regardless of the closed door or what they were doing, they'd hear me if I screamed. Not sure what to say, I looked at his hands. His fingers were long and graceful, and his nails were clean. I thought of how a piano player's hands were always referred to in literature.

"Do you play an instrument?"

"Only a stereo or an eight track," he laughed.

We spent the next hour talking about music. When I told him I liked Jackson Browne, he smiled. "All the girls like Jackson Browne. You should listen to David Bowie. There's no one else like him."

Brian showed up the next weekend and the weekend after that. He worked nights as a busboy in a restaurant, so he came during my lunch break or in the forty-five-minute gap between my job ending and his starting. For the past year, I'd pretty much kept clear of boys, especially older boys. But I liked Brian's attention, and the little gaps of time we spent together felt safe.

Andrea Leeb

When school ended, I added Fridays and Mondays to my work schedule. On the second Friday in June, Brian and I sat on the concrete bridge separating Main Street from the web of canals running through town. I'd finished work for the day, and once again had worn my blue halter dress and sandals. That day the weather cooperated with my outfit. Warm and toasty in the late afternoon sun, I basked in Brian's attention. He was working that night, and looked grown-up and sophisticated dressed in dark slacks and a white shirt and his hair pulled back into a ponytail. In one hand, he held a paper shopping bag. I wondered what was inside.

Couples holding hands, families eating ice cream, and children crying as their parents schlepped them from one store to the next packed the sidewalk in front of us. The traffic on Main Street was bumper-to-bumper with station wagons, Pintos, and muscle cars. Some of them honked their horns as if the sound would make all the other cars magically disappear.

"Funny how they all show up on the same day," I said.

"Summer," Brian shrugged. "I brought you a present." He reached into the bag and pulled out an album.

My cheeks felt hot and my hands shook as I took it: *The Rise and Fall of Ziggy Stardust and the Spiders from Mars*. A blond David Bowie in a blue jumpsuit, a guitar slung over one shoulder, stood in a dark alley. I'd never gotten a present from a boy before. That album turned out to be one of the best gifts I ever received.

"It'll change your life," Brian said. "You'll never listen to Jackson Browne again."

"We'll see." I leaned over and kissed his cheek.

"Our first kiss." He took my hand in his. Then he kissed me for real. I opened my mouth and kissed him back. His mouth tasted like cigarettes and toothpaste. I wanted to kiss him forever.

He had to leave for work a few minutes later, but before we said goodbye, he asked me out. "Some friends are going up to Ringing Rocks next Tuesday. We go up there a lot."

such a pretty picture

Ringing Rocks State Park was about a forty-minute drive up the river in the opposite direction from the blue house where I had driven with Chad the previous summer. I'd never been there, but I'd heard it was in the middle of nowhere.

"Friends?" My chest tightened. "Do they go to your school?"

"Another couple. My friend Ken and his girlfriend Tina."

Hearing the word *couple*, I smiled. "Are we a couple?"

"I hope so," he said, and kissed me again.

For the rest of the summer, it became our thing. Every Tuesday, Wednesday, and Thursday—my three days off—the four of us spent the late mornings and early afternoons driving the winding country roads, smoking pot, and listening to David Bowie in Ken's VW Bug. Ken and Tina sat in the front, and Brian and I in the back. We never wore seat belts, and he'd wrap his arms around me while we rode. There were lots of parks to choose from, but we went to Ringing Rocks the most. A boulder field surrounded by trees, it had fewer people than Bowman's Tower or Washington Crossing. Sometimes the four of us stayed together, but mostly we'd break off into couples. Lying on a flat boulder under the hot summer sun, Brian and I kissed for hours. A summer of swollen lips, my happiest ever. I fell in love, not just with Brian, but with the whole group.

Early in our relationship, I had told Brian that I was a virgin. He assured me we'd take it slow, and for the first couple of months he seemed satisfied with kissing, touching my breasts, and rubbing against me fully clothed. In the beginning of August, he told me he wanted to go further. "I want to make love to you," he said. No boy had ever talked like that to me before. It sounded like something someone would say in a movie or a book.

On our two-month anniversary of dating, as we pulled into the parking lot, Brian whispered in my ear. "Ken and I were up here this weekend. I found an abandoned shed. Let's go there instead of the park."

We arranged to meet Ken and Tina back at the car in three hours.

"Have fun, you guys." Ken brushed his long blond bangs out of his eyes and gave me a wink.

I flushed with shame.

"Ignore him," Brian whispered, and took my hand.

He led me to a small wooden shed that sat a few feet off the road. He tried the door and shook his head. "I opened it on Saturday, but someone must've come back." He grinned. "The window doesn't lock."

He handed me his backpack and I watched him pull the window open and hoist himself inside. I half wished someone would drive up and yell at us for trespassing.

He opened the door for me. "Mademoiselle."

Except for a wooden table with a box of rusty tools, the shed was empty. The air smelled musty and stale. A crust of dirt and dust covered the cement floor. I listened for the sound of mice or squirrels.

"Are you sure this is safe?" The shed reminded me of *Deliverance*.

"I locked the front door and shut the window. If someone comes, we'll hear them." He pulled a washed-out blue blanket out of his backpack.

We lay together on the blanket and kissed. I loved kissing Brian, and part of me wanted to go further. But at the same time, the idea of sex scared me. As he moved his hand down my stomach and began to unbutton my shorts, I pushed him away.

"Relax, I won't hurt you," he said, and kissed me again. I was persuaded.

"I trust you," I said as I unbuttoned my shorts the rest of the way. I wanted to please him, to make him love me.

He helped me wiggle out of my shorts and panties. He pulled his jeans down to his ankles. We both kept our socks on. I had scratches on my hips and lower stomach from cutting myself, but he didn't notice.

such a pretty picture

Still wearing his tank top, Brian climbed on top of me. He touched me and put a finger inside of me. "Relax," he said again. I wanted so badly to feel safe with him. I touched him back, letting him grow hard in my hands. And then I remembered the feeling. I saw my father looming above me. *Go away*, I said to the image. I buried my face in Brian's neck, inhaling his scent. Ivory soap and sweat. But when I took another breath, his scent faded, replaced by the smell of Old Spice and gin.

Keeping my eyes open, I tried to focus on Brian. But instead of his face I saw my father's. My body seized, just like it had done with the blue-eyed boy in the woods.

"Stop." I pushed Brian away with my hands and started to cry.

"What's wrong?" He rolled off me.

"I can't." My chest heaved as my tears became sobs.

We tried again two more times: once more in the shed and once in his bed while his parents were at work. I couldn't let him in. The day after the last time, he called me to break up. "I need a normal girlfriend," he said, "one who isn't afraid to have sex." I hung up the phone without talking. I didn't cry.

I lost my not-so-valued virginity a year later. I was sixteen, and Duff was a twenty-two-year-old drummer. I met him at a party at the Jersey Shore. He had dark, waist-length hair that he wore in a braid and talked about our ancestors' animal spirits. He was an Italian kid from Cherry Hill and I found his pretense mildly amusing. He told me that he and the rest of his band were moving to Los Angeles at the end of the summer. Drunk but not completely wasted, I knew exactly what I was doing when I followed him to an empty bedroom. I'd made out with boys but hadn't tried to have sex with anyone since Brian. I wanted to get it over with—to prove I was normal. Duff seemed like a good bet. Regardless of whether it worked or didn't, I knew I'd never see him again, and

Andrea Leeb

given our six-year age difference he'd keep his mouth shut. That time I didn't see my father and my body didn't seize. Maybe I was just drunk enough, or maybe I just stopped caring. The only thing I remember about the sex was that my period started at the exact moment of penetration.

chapter 26

On an early June morning, the air came warm and quiet through an open window. I blinked my eyes awake. I lay in a strange bed with a strange boy. His legs were wrapped around me and our hands clasped together. I shifted, and the boy held me closer. Snuggling against him, I shut my eyes and drifted back to a half sleep.

Ten, maybe fifteen minutes later, the sound of a rooster crowing jolted me awake again. I looked at my watch. "Shit." I jumped out of bed.

"What's wrong?" The boy sat up on his elbows. Lanky, with chestnut brown hair, he reminded me of Jackson Browne. He even had a guitar in the corner of his room.

"It's after five. I told you that I live with my parents. I can't believe I fell asleep."

"I musta worn you out." The boy smiled at me.

Don't flatter yourself, I thought, and reached down to pull my skirt and halter top off the floor.

I was seventeen. I'd met the boy at a community college graduation barbecue the night before. The party had been thrown by two of the boy's roommates, both of whom had been in my calculus class at the college. I had left high school the year before, at the end of my sophomore year, and started going to the college full-time. A compromise worked out between my parents and my high school guidance counselor after my parents refused to let me go to the fancy New England private school I'd secretly applied to.

"I am going to be fucked," I said as I searched for my shoes and my purse, both of which I found a few minutes later under a chair in the far corner of the room. "I'm out of here." I opened the bedroom door and turned to give the Jackson Browne boy a wave.

"I'll call you soon." The boy winked at me in a way that made the downy hair on my arms stand on edge.

"Sure, you will." I closed the door behind me without pointing out that he didn't have my phone number.

Not that I cared. Since the first time with Duff, with the right combination of pot and alcohol, sex had become easier. I can't say I really enjoyed it, but I craved male attention. I also preferred the idea of sleeping with strangers to having a boyfriend. Pretending to be a sexy character in a book by Anaïs Nin or Colette was a lot simpler than faking the normalcy required to sustain a relationship. *A spy in the house of love*, I told myself. And although my body often ran cold, the lust of the boys I'd slept with made me feel validated, desired, and most importantly, in control.

The Jackson Browne boy and his roommates lived in a ramshackle farmhouse about thirty minutes from my parents' house. When I'd arrived the night before, the grass leading up to the house had been covered with cars. Now, my red Chevy Vega sat alone on the tire-marked lawn. The only other cars left were parked in the driveway, presumably belonging to the boy and his calculus roommates.

The grass under my feet was squishy, and my Dr. Scholl's sandals sank into the ground as I walked. Slipping them off, I climbed into the car and started the engine. Above me the predawn sky turned from navy to pale blue, and the moon, which had been full and bright the previous night, faded to an outline.

"Okay, Mama, we have to book," I said out loud, pressing a bare foot on the pedal. "My life depends on it."

such a pretty picture

That morning as I sped toward New Hope, I worried about the scene that waited for me at home. I had no doubt my father would be pissed, but the question was how pissed. Since I'd started at the community college, he pretty much treated me like an unwanted houseguest. Except for the occasional threat to lock me up, he avoided me. Overall, my life was better, but I'd never stayed out all night before and I worried he'd try to take my Vega away. I wasn't a car person but I loved my red Vega. It was my chariot to freedom until I was old enough to leave home for real. It made it possible for me to attend community college and to work evenings as a nursing assistant at New Manor nursing home. If he took it away, my life as I knew it would be over.

I'd bought the car at the end of the previous summer. I'd planned to go alone to the dealership, but my father had insisted on taking me. "A car dealer will take one look at you and sell you the worst clunker on the lot."

It was a gummy August day. A seersucker-suited salesman led my father and me through rows of used cars in various states of decay. I'd worn a pink eyelet blouse and white painter pants. My father, who had by then shaved his sideburns and thrown out his polyester bell-bottoms, was dressed in khaki Bermuda shorts and an Izod polo shirt. Walking side by side, we looked like a normal, middle-class father and daughter.

"This one's a real beauty." The man pointed to a maroon Pontiac Catalina. An ugly houseboat of a car that looked like one of the cars my grandfather owned when I was six or seven.

As I watched my father inspect the car, a river of disappointment rose up in my gut. *Please don't make me buy this one*, I prayed. Although I was responsible for paying for whatever I bought, I knew the ultimate decision was up to my father.

"It's a gas hog," my father said. "She needs something small and safe." He watched the salesman walk toward a white VW Bug. "But not German." My parents, both children during WWII, had not forgiven Germany for the Holocaust and never bought anything made in Germany.

I was the one who spotted the Vega. "What about that car?" I asked. It sat three rows up. A candy-apple-red, two-door hatchback. It glistened like lip gloss in the hot sun.

"Good choice, young lady." The salesman turned to my father. "American made and only two years old. I know it's hard to believe, but the previous owner was a little old lady. She nursed her like a baby."

My father smirked at him. "Do you want to test-drive it, cutie?"

Without answering, I walked over and studied the price sticker in the window. Eleven hundred dollars. I only had seven hundred. "It's too expensive," I mumbled.

"There's wiggle room, and we offer a payment plan," the salesman said to my father.

My father ignored him. "Test-drive it. If you like it, we can come up with a private plan." He gave me a wink.

Seeing that wink, I shivered. "I don't know," I said, my shoulders tensing at the thought of a private plan.

"Consider it an early Chanukah and birthday present."

I remembered my Christmas morning bicycle, a late Chanukah/early birthday present. A bike that had cost me a chunk of my childhood. I knew better than to make private deals with my father. I stayed quiet.

"Your mother and I agreed," he said.

"Mommy knows?" I let my body relax.

"You know I don't keep secrets from your mother." He gave me a broad grin.

We bought the car that day for a thousand dollars cash. I figured as long as my mother knew, I was safe to take my father's gift. Despite everything, at seventeen I was still hopeful enough

such a pretty picture

to trust my mother. The only catch was that my father insisted on joint ownership. "For insurance," he said, and gave me another wink.

When I arrived home from the Jackson Browne boy's house, I parked at the bottom of the gravel driveway. Inside the house the shades were all drawn, so I couldn't tell if anyone was up. As I opened the side door, I slipped off my shoes and checked my watch. It was only six o'clock. If I was lucky they'd still be asleep.

"Andrea." I heard my mother's voice before I closed the door. "We're in the kitchen."

My father sat at the table dressed in a T-shirt and shorts, nursing a cup of coffee. His morning newspaper sat folded and untouched in front of him. My mother stood behind him, ironing.

The room smelled of coffee and starch. For a few seconds they stared at me without talking.

"Where were you?" My father narrowed his eyes and shot me one of his killer looks. I stood in front of them, my jaw clenched and my stomach shaking.

"I was up all night worried," my mother said.

A little late for that, I wanted to say. "I stayed at Patty's. The party ended after midnight and I didn't want to wake you."

"Bullshit." My father slammed a fist against the wooden table. "I know what you're up to. You parade around half-naked with that red lipstick and those cheap bracelets. You dress like a Forty-Second Street hooker and act like a cat on a hot tin roof." He stood up, looming over me with his height.

I glanced down at myself. My halter top covered my cleavage and my gauzy skirt was long and flowing. In my mind, I was dressed more like Stevie Nicks than Maggie the Cat.

"Don't talk to me like that," I said, standing straight and

staring directly into his eyes. I wanted him to know I was no longer a twelve-year-old girl who was too afraid to speak up. *You are not the only one with insurance*, I thought.

"You are lucky I don't lock you away until you learn how to control your impulses." Spit formed at the corner of his mouth. "I'm ashamed to be your father. Get out of my sight before I smack you."

I didn't move.

"You heard your father." My mother put the iron down and pursed her lips.

To my surprise, Sarai was already up and waiting for me in my bedroom. Over the past several years we'd grown apart. I was busy with school and my job and she with her best friend, Jacquie.

"He's a dick." Sarai sat on my bed with her legs crossed meditation-style. She was still dressed in her pajamas and one of my mother's old silk robes. Although she was only fourteen, she had already started lightening her honey-colored hair. It fell in pale blonde waves around her face.

"I should have called or come home."

"Doesn't change that he's a dick."

I shrugged. "Most fathers would have been pissed."

"Most fathers don't say their daughter looks like a hooker and acts like a cat on a tin roof. Whatever that means."

"It's from a play," I said. "By Tennessee Williams."

"Who cares? It's a dick thing to say." She pulled a crumpled cigarette out of her pocket. "Wanna share?"

I nodded, opened my bedroom window, and then turned back to her.

"Wait to light it. I need to get my ashtray out of the closet."

Sarai laughed and pulled my desk chair in front of the window. "You are so uptight," she said and climbed outside.

such a pretty picture

Our house was a Dutch Colonial, and my bedroom window opened to the lower, flatter roof. On hot summer days, Sarai and I would slather ourselves with baby oil and lay outside. That morning, we sat with our backs against my window and our legs stretched out in front of us.

"You think he'll take your car away?" Sarai cupped her hand around the cigarette to light it.

"Nope. He doesn't want to start with me."

She inhaled and then blew two smoke rings. "He likes you better. Did you know he tried to break a plate over my head last week?"

"He tried to break a plate over your head," I repeated, incredulous.

"You were at work. I missed my curfew, but I was only a few minutes late. *Saturday Night Live* had just started."

She handed me the cigarette. It was slightly crushed and I had to hold it past the filter to keep it from breaking.

"He was drunk," Sarai continued. "It was one of those old plastic plates. The white ones from when we lived in Winter Park. He hit me so hard it made my ears ring."

"Did you tell Mom?"

"She was sitting at the kitchen table. She saw the whole thing."

I closed my eyes for a second and shook my head: *Nothing changes.*

"Guess what she said?"

I took a drag of the cigarette.

"She told me to be grateful it wasn't glass."

"Why didn't you tell me?"

She stared at me and our eyes met. It hit me that her once chocolate pudding eyes had turned hard. They reminded me of brown pebbles. "What could you have done about it?" She ground the cigarette into the ashtray.

Andrea Leeb

Without answering, I moved the ashtray and draped my arm around her. She nestled against me and I hugged her tighter. In front of us two squirrels chased each other up and down a towering oak tree.

chapter 27

I left home and went to college at Georgetown University in Washington, DC. Freedom. Away from my parents, I could finally breathe. Sarai left at the same time. My mother had decided she should go to boarding school. Her decision was odd—made odder because of my parents' earlier refusal of my request to go to private school. The inequity infuriated me, but at the same time I felt relieved that I didn't have to leave Sarai alone in that angry house.

I made friends the way young people do in college. Girls and boys. Some for life and others until graduation. My junior year, I even had a boyfriend.

Surprising my parents and myself, I majored in nursing and not English or literature. Most of my friends were English or history majors, with a few in the School of Foreign Service. Still a compulsive reader and perennially insecure, I told my friends I chose nursing after reading *Man's Fate*, André Malraux's book about the Chinese revolution. "I want to be a useful proletariat when the revolution comes here," I said over bongs and beer. A pretentious, bullshit answer, I could have just as easily told them I'd based my decision on hours of watching *M*A*S*H*. A more honest answer, but still not exactly the truth.

The real reason embarrassed me. It felt too trite for my smart friends with their private school educations. I'd decided to become a nurse because I wanted to help people heal. I remembered that day in the hospital when a nurse hugged my mother, giving her a moment of comfort as she looked at her sick child. In moments of despair, I wanted to give people that same flash of hope. Something no one had ever given me.

I also wanted to be independent. In the late seventies and early eighties, there was a nursing shortage. I knew that when I graduated, I would (unlike my liberal arts friends) easily find a job. My independence came more quickly than I expected. Sophomore year, I applied for and received a full National Health Service scholarship: tuition and a monthly stipend in return for a commitment to spend three years after graduation working for the Public Health Service. Completely self-supporting, I no longer had to ask my parents for anything. I felt invincible.

Ten days before graduation, after two a.m. on a warm May night when Key Bridge was empty except for the occasional taxi, I walked on the footpath from Arlington, Virginia, toward DC. In one hand, I carried a pair of red stilettos I'd purchased at a vintage store earlier that day. My permed hair fell down my back in a mass of curls. Behind me, I heard the footsteps of the two boys I was with. We were dressed in our version of adult clothing, the boys in dark jeans, white shirts, and skinny ties and me in a black dress with a tight waist and a tulle skirt. We were on our way home from a graduation party at an Arlington hotel. Having spent most of our collective money at the hotel bar, we'd decided to walk the mile across the bridge into Georgetown. I'd known both boys since we were sophomores. Casual friends, we'd hung out loosely with the same group of people off and on.

I had returned to DC a few days before, having spent the last semester of my senior year in England. I'd been—or thought I'd been—fine when I was abroad, but as I stepped out of National

Airport, something broke. I felt as if the cocoon of shame buried deep inside of me had inexplicably split open. I began to see my father's face in flashes, to remember his smell of Old Spice and gin, to feel his hands touching my body in places a father should never touch. In the days that followed, after years of freedom, the flashes came without warning. As if my subconscious was a tank of toxic memories that needed a moment of release.

That night, the flashes hit me in rapid succession, like lightning or bullets from a machine gun. My body shrank from the pain, and I began to cry. Halfway across the bridge, I stopped walking and leaned against the railing. "I want to jump," I whispered as I dropped my shoes. A moonless night, the river was illuminated by the lights lining the path and the city in the distance. The dark water looked still and calm. It called to me with a promise of peace. The railing did not seem insurmountable. *I can climb this*, I thought. Holding the railing with both hands, I lifted my right leg toward the top. I could see myself: flying, falling, plunging. I imagined the feeling of the cold water rushing into my body, flooding my lungs, and soothing the hole in my heart until there was nothing left of me.

"Stop!" From behind, the shorter of the two boys grabbed my arm. His nails punctured my flesh.

"Leave me alone." I twisted out of his grip, pushing my body against the railing.

"Andrea!" The other boy, taller and broader than the first, yanked my shoulders back. Losing my footing, I fell into him. He pulled me around to face him. His normally sunny expression seemed deflated. I saw the confusion in his eyes. I looked over at the shorter boy. He stared at the ground, refusing to look at me. They both seemed so helpless and scared. Young. If I'd jumped, it would have scarred them for life.

Andrea Leeb

~ ~ ~

At the time, I was crashing with friends in a five-bedroom Glover Park rental. I was using a bedroom that one of their roommates had just abandoned for the summer. When I got home, my friends were sleeping. I didn't tell them about the bridge, and the two boys I had been with promised me they would never breathe a word to anyone.

I thought I would be okay, but over the next ten days, I fell into a deep depression. It was Senior Week, but instead of participating in the festivities, I lay in my bed and cried. My body ached in ways that I had never imagined. The soles of my feet throbbed and any step caused me pain. When I brushed my teeth the bristles from the toothbrush felt like needles piercing my gums. After a week or so, my eyes went dry, the flashes subsided and the pain dissipated, and I became mercifully numb—too anesthetized to feel any shame. The depression consumed me, an unrelenting surge of black water. Wave after wave. I no longer wanted to kill myself. I was already dead.

The afternoon before graduation, my parents drove the five hours from New Hope to DC, and Sarai took the train from Manhattan, where she had just finished her freshman year of college. My parents had gotten two rooms at a hotel in Dupont Circle. The plan had been for my mother and sister to meet me at the house, and then we would walk into Georgetown, do some shopping, and meet my father for dinner. Although it was after one p.m., I was in bed when the doorbell rang.

My mother stood at the door dressed in a black summer silk and flats. She still wore her hair short and gamine-style. She wasn't wearing much jewelry, just her wedding ring and a strand

such a pretty picture

of black pearls—a Mother's Day gift from my father, she'd told me. Although it was a few months before her forty-second birthday, she looked young enough to pass for a graduate student. My sister stood next to her in high-waisted Jordache jeans and a white tank, with a midriff-cut denim jacket slung over her shoulder. She had lost the freshman fifteen she'd put on her first semester and had recently cut her long hair into a blunt, chin-length bob. Despite the DC humidity, the two of them looked fresh. They could have been posing for a mother-daughter photo spread in *Glamour* magazine.

"Why aren't you dressed?" my mother said, taking in my Medusa hair, the oversized, wrinkled white T-shirt, and the running shorts I had been wearing nonstop for the past seven days. "We came all this way and you're not ready." Her face wrinkled with displeasure as she took a step inside.

Sarai followed her, stopping to hug me. She was wearing a flowery perfume I recognized as Chloé. As we hugged, I became conscious of my own sour smell. "You look like shit," she whispered.

The front door of the house led directly into the living room. I watched my mother take in the scattered newspapers and overflowing ashtrays and saw her eyes fall on a bong in the middle of the coffee table. She pursed her lips and then she turned to face me and took my hand. "We need to talk." I shivered. Her hand felt warm and soft: motherly. A hand that, after all these years, I still craved.

In my temporary room, my mother and sister sat, shoulders touching, on the single bed. I sat across from them on an empty blue milk crate. I had several mosquito bites on my left leg and I had scratched them open without noticing. A thin rivulet of blood ran down my calf.

"Is it a guy?" Sarai looked at me.

I sighed. "Not a guy." My tongue felt crusty. I wished they would leave so I could go back to bed.

"Then what? I have never seen you like this. You're scaring me."

My mother spoke before I could answer. "Kevin called me," she said, referring to the most mature of my temporary housemates. "He told me what happened."

"When did he call?" The boys I had been with on the bridge had promised not to tell anyone, but they must have told Kevin. I wondered who else they'd told.

"He called me last Tuesday. He told me you threatened to jump off a bridge."

"He wasn't there," I said, summoning the single bead of energy I had left. "He had no right to call you."

My mother met my eyes. "I thought he was exaggerating or that you were being overdramatic. A ploy for attention."

Was that really what she thought? Was she right? I closed my eyes and pressed my finger pads against my lids. I could see the calm black water glistening and hear it whispering my name. *No, it hadn't been a ploy. At that moment I had wanted to die.*

"You tried to jump off a bridge?" Sarai interrupted.

"Keep your voice down," my mother said. "And she threatened, not tried. There is a big difference."

Opening my eyes, I looked at my mother. She was twisting her pearls tightly around her neck. *She doesn't believe a word of what she's saying but she'll never admit it.*

"Why didn't anyone call me?" Sarai asked. "Why am I always the last to know?"

"This isn't about you."

Listening to them, my ears began to ring. "I didn't want to upset you," I said to Sarai.

"You think seeing you like this isn't upsetting?"

"I'm sorry," I croaked. *Please leave. I need to sleep.*

"Enough." My mother stood up. "Talking about the past only makes it worse. Trust me, I know." She pulled me up next to her and wrapped her arms around me.

such a pretty picture

Collapsing into her, I began to weep little girl tears. "I'm sorry," I said again.

"Shush . . . shush," my mother whispered, rocking me. The last time she had rocked me like that, I was eleven, a few days after I'd been released from the hospital. As she rocked me now, I had a sliver of clarity: My mother was able to love me only if I was broken, and the more broken the better.

"I have to be in Arizona by the end of the summer," I said, and took a step away from her. If I defaulted on my scholarship commitment to serve, I would have to pay back four times the amount of money that had been given to me.

"Don't worry," my mother said. "You can come home for the summer and rest."

I felt my body go still. I no longer considered my parents' house my home. When I left for college, I had promised myself I'd never live there again. The longest I'd stayed since I started college was a four-day weekend. The idea of moving back, even for a couple months, felt like the ultimate failure. And what if I didn't get better? What if I got stuck there forever? Just thinking about it made me wish I'd had the courage to jump.

"I don't know," I muttered.

"You can stay with me," Sarai volunteered.

I shook my head. Sarai had just moved out of the dorm and into a one-bedroom apartment with a roommate. She was working full-time that summer and had a brand-new boyfriend and a dog. A sister that looked like shit was the last thing she needed.

"Look, Ange, you can't stay here," my mother said. "Your friends don't want you. They asked me to take you home."

I winced. "I guess I don't have a choice." I closed my eyes and rubbed my face.

She took my hands from my face and held them again. "I promise everything will be fine." She tightened her grip. "We can leave right after graduation. You will be going to your commencement, right?"

"Yes," I mumbled, although I wasn't sure how.

"Good." Letting go of my hands, she took a step back. "Your father would be so disappointed if you didn't walk." She rubbed her hands together as if she were washing them clean.

chapter 28

Arriving at my parents' house, I went straight to my old bedroom and locked the door behind me. With my comforter pulled over my head and my body curled into a fetal position, I slept for the next two days, ignoring my mother's knocking. I ventured out only to pee or grab the pitcher of water she'd left in front of my door. On the third day, she became insistent.

"I'm not leaving," I heard her say outside my door.

With a sigh, I pushed myself out of bed and let her in.

"Come sit in the gazebo with me. It's a beautiful day, and I made iced tea and bought cookies from the bakery in town."

"I'm not hungry. Just let me sleep a little more. I'll come downstairs tomorrow."

She shook her head. "We need to talk."

Following her, my bones felt heavy. I lumbered down the stairs, walking as if I had ten-pound weights on my wrists and ankles.

The white wooden gazebo sat a few feet from the house. Surrounded by rosebushes, it overlooked a cliff of ivy and trees. Barefoot and wearing one of my mother's silk robes, I sat down on one of the two wicker rocking chairs. My mother, dressed in a crisp white cotton shift and silver sandals, placed a plate of cookies and a pitcher of iced tea on the coffee table in front of us.

She sat down and handed me the plate. Madeleine cookies, shell-shaped and sprinkled with white powder. "These always make me think of Proust," she said.

I wasn't hungry, but I took one so she wouldn't drive me crazy. My mother and I both loved madeleine cookies. That day, the lemon butter cookies tasted like paste to me. I slumped in my chair.

"I know what you're going through," she said. "I've been through it."

My mind went straight to the bath and my mother's blindness. It was a conversation I had both prayed for and dreaded. Thinking about it made me dizzy, and I closed my eyes to stop the spinning.

"I had just started my freshman year in high school. I couldn't eat and I vacillated between insomnia and sleeping for days. My mother sent me to a psychiatrist."

"Nanny did?" *Thank God she isn't going to talk about her blindness.*

"It's surprising, but sometimes she could be quite modern."

"How long did you see him or her?"

"Him, for three years."

Momentarily jolted out of my own depression, I sat up straight. "For three years? Why don't I know this? Why didn't you tell me when you made me see Dr. W?"

"You were too young. It's not the kind of thing a mother tells a young child."

"Why did you stop seeing him?"

"I got better and I got engaged."

"Did Dad know?"

"I don't keep secrets from your father."

Hearing her say that, my temples began to throb.

"He even met him," she said.

"Your psychiatrist met Dad?" The conversation had veered off course. I was relieved that we weren't talking about me, but my mother never confided her secrets. I wasn't sure what to think.

"The psychiatrist insisted. He had him come to his office a few weeks after we got engaged."

such a pretty picture

"How did that go?" I took a sip of iced tea. I wanted to fish out the ice cubes and hold them against my head, but my mother would have had a fit.

"He told me not to marry your father. 'Marlene,' he said, 'that young man is very disturbed. If you marry him, he will destroy you.'"

Now I wanted to cry. It was one more warning about my father in a lifetime of warnings that my mother ignored. If she'd listened to it, I wouldn't have been born. I should have been glad she resisted. But that a psychiatrist had seen something so obvious in my father after meeting him once terrified me.

"Thank God, I ignored him," my mother said. "I never set foot in his office again." She paused. "You're the first person I've ever told this to. Your father would've been crushed."

"Crushed by what?"

"If I'd told him what the psychiatrist said. Daddy is very sensitive."

Sensitive. I blanched hearing the word. "Did you ever think about breaking up with him?" Two yellow jackets landed on the cookies, but I didn't have the strength to swat at them.

"Never. Your father is a complicated man, but he is my one true love. There is nothing anyone could say or anything he could do to make me leave him." She was repeating the mantra I'd been hearing for years.

I began to sweat. The summer heat felt oppressive. Closing my eyes, I put my head between my legs. *I don't have the stamina for this conversation*, I thought. *Not now, maybe not ever.*

"Are you okay?"

"Tired," I said, sitting up again.

My mother's eyes fell on the bees. "I keep telling your father we need to get screens." She shooed them away but they were back in a heartbeat. "I don't know how I got off on that tangent." She paused again. "I know you don't want to hear this, but you need to see a psychiatrist. It's the only way you'll snap out of this."

"I don't have time for three years of therapy. I have to be in Arizona in three months."

"Not for therapy. For medication. I found a doctor who specializes in psychopharmacology. He says it's common for young people—people your age—to have some physiological depression. Especially after big events like graduation and coming home from England."

"He's not supposed to talk to you without my consent." I thought about Dr. W. The last thing I wanted was another psychiatrist who thought he had the right to talk about me with my parents.

"We spoke in hypotheticals."

"My graduation and my coming home from England are not hypotheticals."

"There are new pills to treat depression. You could be feeling better in two or three weeks."

"I just need to sleep."

"I made an appointment for this Friday. His office is in the city. I'll drive you." Her voice faltered. "Please."

"If I say yes, can I go back to bed?" The conversation had depleted me. I wanted to forget it, to wrap myself in my comforter and sleep until everything vanished.

Dr. K was in his mid-sixties, he had diplomas from three Ivy League colleges on his wall, and wore pinstripe shirts with French cuffs and gold cuff links. My mother came with me for my first few visits. The pills he gave me, a precursor to Prozac, worked quickly. By the end of June, I felt better.

As the fog lifted, the pain returned. No longer excruciating, but it felt like a gnawing ache deep in my chest. I tried to distract myself. I cut my hair short and spiky and dyed it black. I gave up eating meat and got a part-time job at a local nursing home. On my nights off, I went to punk clubs in Trenton with an old high school friend.

such a pretty picture

My father had not touched me in ten years and I hadn't lived in my parents' house for the past four. That summer, as if by unspoken agreement, we stayed out of each other's way.

Even so, living under the same roof tested me. The memories were stubborn and refused to be suppressed. Seeing my father exacerbated them. Sometimes, as I'd wander into the kitchen, I'd find him drinking his morning coffee and reading the *New York Times*. Watching him, I'd remember the smell of gin on his breath, his Santa hat askew and the touch of his hands on my five-year-old body.

The onslaught of depression had terrified me. And although it had lifted, the memories made me feel as if I were dancing on the precipice of going through it again. I didn't think I could tolerate another siege. *Maybe I needed more than a pill? Maybe I needed someone to talk to? Maybe I needed therapy?* A few days before our last visit, I decided to tell Dr. K the truth. During my appointments, he'd only asked me about my physical symptoms. But he was, I reasoned, a psychiatrist; he had been trained how to talk to people. I thought he would understand or, at the very least, help me find a therapist in Arizona.

"You're feeling better?" Dr. K asked me now.

"Yes, definitely better, but I'm scared."

"It's to be expected. You've been through a lot this summer." He picked up his prescription pad and pen. "I'll give you a prescription to last you until December."

"There's something I wanted to talk about."

"Yes?"

One, two, three seconds passed. My body trembled. *Tell him*, I thought. *Just tell him.*

"When I was younger, my father touched me." I shut my eyes for a split second.

"Touched you?"

"My vagina." Saying the word *vagina* to this man with his

starched shirts and fancy cuff links left a dirty taste in my mouth. I felt like a twelve-year-old girl again.

"When did that happen?" he asked. He clicked his pen and leaned toward me. I wanted to disappear.

As I met his eyes, I knew I'd made a mistake. "The first time, I was four and a half."

"That's very young." He held his pen without writing. "Where did this touching occur?"

"In the bathtub." I wished I'd kept it to myself.

"Ah." He nodded and leaned back in his chair. "There can be times when a parent is washing a child and their hand or the washcloth can accidentally brush the child's vagina. This accidental touch might feel good to the child. But later, the memory can be confusing, especially for adolescent girls and young women."

Listening to him, my body became rigid. *I'm not confused*, I wanted to scream at him. *And why aren't you asking me about the other times? There's years and years of touching.* But I knew it was pointless. No matter what I said, this man wouldn't or didn't want to believe me.

"I've never met your father," he said, "but your mother is a lovely woman. She was so concerned when she brought you here. I find it hard to believe she'd allow something that awful to happen to you."

I nodded, giving him the affirmation he wanted.

He put his pen and pad down. "As I said, young women often get confused."

I stared out the window directly into the blinding afternoon sun.

"Confused," I whispered.

"It happens frequently. Nothing to be ashamed of."

I took a breath and held it for a beat. Exhaling, I closed my eyes and promised myself once again that I would never tell anyone. This time, I'd bury my secrets for good. If I buried them long enough and deep enough, then maybe they'd disappear forever.

Part Three
1989-1992

chapter 29

On a Saturday morning in mid-February of 1990, I walked upstairs to the second-floor loft of the apartment I shared with my boyfriend, Christopher. Directly above our kitchen, we used the loft as an office. I stopped in front of a locked file cabinet tucked into the corner. My hands shook as I unlocked the top drawer and pulled out a black cardboard box.

Back downstairs, I set the box on our kitchen table next to my electric typewriter and an application from the New York State Bar Association. In 1986, at twenty-eight, I'd decided to make a career change from nursing to law—a change prompted by years of what I viewed as disrespect from male doctors and a desire to be taken more seriously. I wanted to find my voice. In 1989, on the same day as the Tiananmen Square uprising, I graduated from law school with honors.

The application was a detailed background check meant to prove or disprove my moral fitness to practice law. It asked me to list every school I attended, every address where I'd lived, and every job I'd held, as well as to respond to a litany of other questions. I had taken the bar exam in July right after graduation and had been notified in November that I'd passed. Most of my friends from law school had filled out their moral fitness paperwork right after the bar exam, and the rest once we were told we'd passed. Only the procrastinators delayed. And me, a person who slept with her watch on and had never turned a paper in late.

such a pretty picture

That morning, I couldn't put it off any longer; the firm where I worked had been asking about my admission status. Christopher was in Atlantic City at a bachelor party for another investment banker. I had the apartment to myself until Sunday evening. Opening the box, I pulled out four manila folders stuffed with documents. As I picked up the first folder, my hands began to shake again: an unreasonable reaction. On paper, my life looked great. A simple background check should not create so much angst. But for me, any excavation of my life was excruciating.

I put the first page of the application into the typewriter. Our apartment—technically Christopher's, although I paid him rent—was, except for the bedroom and the loft, a large open space with floor-to-ceiling windows. I sat with my back to the kitchen facing the street. Outside, the sky threatened snow. Imagining the cold, I shivered and pulled up the hood of my sweatshirt.

I flew through the beginning of the application. *This isn't so bad*, I thought. Then, almost on cue, I got to the section marked legal actions. The instructions read *List any lawsuits whether plaintiff or defendant, including any actions related to paternity, child support, or divorce.* I pulled a sealed envelope out of the folder. Taking a deep breath, I opened it and took out the document inside: *Petition Granting Divorce*. I had not looked at it in over six years. I never talked about the divorce to anyone. Out of all the people in my life at the time, only Sarai, my parents, and a couple of longtime girlfriends knew about that marriage.

Geoff and I met at an Iggy Pop concert in Phoenix. Twenty-one years old and long-limbed with dyed red hair, he had dropped out of college and worked part-time at a record store. I was twenty-three and had just transferred to the Phoenix Indian Medical Center. At first, we based our relationship on smoking pot, listening to punk rock, and going to concerts. Three months in,

Andrea Leeb

Geoff became ill with what we thought was a blood disease. We got married because we were scared. He was scared of dying, and I was afraid of the night. The flashbacks of my father had abated, but I still lived in constant fear of being attacked, waiting for a man to appear out of nowhere. Each night, I'd move my coffee table and push my couch in front of the door. Even with the barricade, I slept well only with somebody next to me. It didn't matter who.

We got married at City Hall, the clerks our only witnesses. I wore a white dress from the 1920s I'd found in a thrift store and carried a bouquet of daisies. A few weeks before, I had shaved my hair up the sides and painted every other strand yellow and burgundy. I ratted it on top like the girls in the band Bananarama. Geoff dressed in black jeans, a new white T-shirt, and a motorcycle jacket. He'd buzzed the red out of his hair. That day, he reminded me of a hazel-eyed James Dean. Over the next few months, he fell in love. I tried, but I couldn't love him back. At least not the way he loved me.

We were married for a little over ten months, and then I left him (although we stayed married for another year so he could keep my health insurance). By then the doctors had discovered that Geoff's illness had been caused by a reaction to the red hair dye. So long as he never dyed his hair red again, he would get better.

After Geoff, I bounced from one short relationship to another. I wasn't looking for love, just the perception of protection and a body to sleep next to. Someone to keep the boogeyman at bay.

I studied the petition, then typed in the date of our divorce: May 23, 1984. As I slid the petition back into its envelope, I heard the freight elevator grinding to a stop outside of the apartment. Our floor was split into two loft apartments. An actor with a chocolate Lab lived next to us. He had another house in Westchester and rarely stayed in the city on weekends. I had seen him leaving on Thursday. *Fuck*, I thought. *If someone breaks in would anyone hear me scream?* Tiptoeing into the kitchen, I pulled out a chef's knife. The elevator door clanked closed. Waiting for the sound of a knock or a crowbar prying the lock open, I stood with both hands gripping the knife handle. Then the dog barked twice. I relaxed but brought the knife back to the table—just in case.

Knife by my side, I sat for a few minutes catching my breath. The application taunted me in my typewriter. I wished I could snap my fingers and stop my trip down memory lane. But instead, I pulled out another envelope. Inside it, another petition granting another divorce.

At the time I met Charlie, I was working as a nurse and planning to apply to law school. A graphic designer, he had collar-length brown hair, green eyes, and a long thin face. He reminded me of a Spanish nobleman in an El Greco painting. Not handsome, but he had a downtown cool and was the best dance partner I'd ever had. We got married the summer after we met. This time I had a wedding: a hundred people and a rockabilly band at Chez Odette, a famous French restaurant in New Hope.

I didn't love Charlie either—not the way a wife is supposed to love a husband. The night before the wedding, I sat alone at my parents' kitchen table. In the center, my mother had placed a vase filled with freshly cut lilacs. The sweet smell permeated the air. Charlie and I were staying with my parents until the wedding. He'd gone to pick up his family and Sarai, who were all spending the night at a local hotel. My parents, Nanny, and I were supposed to meet them shortly for the rehearsal dinner.

I was already dressed in my pre-bride clothing: a flowy cream-colored dress and a long strand of pearls. My parents and Nanny were upstairs getting ready. My mother had left her car keys on the kitchen counter. I stared at them, wondering what everyone would do if I got in her car and drove away. A runaway bride in a dark blue Subaru station wagon: an impossible thought. I turned my attention to my nails; Sarai and I had gone for a manicure earlier. They were painted ballet slipper pink, the polish brides always seemed to wear. I hated the color and wished I'd kept my usual blood-red. Staring at the keys again, I slipped off my engagement ring. My empty finger felt light and free.

"Hi, cutie." My father interrupted my thoughts and sat down across from me.

I recoiled from the endearment.

He frowned. "You don't seem happy."

"Just nervous," I said, and put my ring back on.

"Are you sure?"

"Sure?"

"About the wedding? Charlie?"

I hardly ever spent time with my father. I wondered how he knew what I was feeling and if that knowledge meant that we were alike. I shuddered at the thought.

"You don't need to go through with this," he said. "We could cancel it."

My eyes began to sting. Earlier, I had applied layers of mascara, and I didn't want to cry. I took a deep breath to will the tears away. "It's too late."

"I'm sorry." He touched my hand.

I pulled my hand away and stared at him, wondering what he meant. *Was he sorry I was marrying a man I didn't love? Or was he sorry for the things he had done to me that led me to this moment?* Maybe it was both. I didn't know. I didn't ask. It was the only time my father ever apologized to me for anything.

I started law school in New York City the fall after our wedding and left Charlie at the beginning of my second year. We were together just long enough to unfreeze the slice of wedding cake

such a pretty picture

saved for our first anniversary. Like Geoff, he loved me absolutely, but by the time I left I could barely touch him.

"I can't believe you're doing this." He stood wet-faced in the doorway of our bedroom and watched while I packed my clothing into two suitcases.

"You can keep everything. All the wedding presents and the furniture."

"I don't want the wedding presents."

"Then sell them." I went back to my packing. I knew I'd hurt him but I had to leave. And truthfully, I was too damaged to care.

Besides, I had another boyfriend waiting. I met Seth in our law school student break room. We had no classes in common, but we studied together every night. After leaving the library, he'd walk me across town from the West Village, where our law school was, to the East Village, where Charlie and I lived, always careful to separate a block before my apartment. I told myself I wasn't cheating, but emotionally I knew that was a lie.

Seth and I hooked up a few days after I left Charlie. We stayed together for eighteen months. At first, I liked him more than he liked me. After I graduated, things changed. Seth seemed to grow into our relationship. My cue to leave. When I broke up with him, he acted surprised but didn't cry. Neither did I, because by then I was already interviewing candidates for my next relationship. A few weeks later, I met Christopher.

The divorces done, I finished the rest of the application. The smell of garlic wafted through the apartment. My neighbor must have been cooking. I checked my watch—after six, and I hadn't eaten all day.

Christopher and I had our second date a few days before Christmas. We'd gone to a matinee at a small playhouse in the West Village. We were both dressed in black jeans and black cashmere turtleneck sweaters. "Twins," we'd laughed when we'd taken off our coats. Tall and lean with honey-colored hair, a chiseled face, and gold-flecked hazel eyes, even dressed casually Christopher looked elegant. Infatuated, I spent most of the play sneaking glances at him. Afterward he walked me home. The sun had just begun to set, and the streets glittered with Christmas lights. Our breath hung in the air while we walked. Neither of us was wearing gloves. After a block or two, he took my hand. A surge of electricity passed between us. He stopped walking and brought my hand to his lips.

"You're perfect," he whispered. "Your hair, your clothes, your body, even the length of your nails. Everything perfect."

"Perfect." I said the word out loud as I slipped out of my daydream. Picking up the black box, I walked upstairs and put it safely into my file cabinet. Then, silver key in hand, I twisted the lock shut with a click.

chapter 30

I gripped the silver pole in the center of the packed subway car as the train rumbled downtown. Weighted down—a tote bag on one shoulder and my briefcase hanging from the other—I swayed with the rhythm of the train to keep my balance. It was an unseasonable, seventy-degree February day. The subway car felt like a sauna and reeked of perfume, sweat, and a hint of urine.

It had been a year since I'd submitted my moral fitness application to the New York Bar Association. Fully admitted, I had just left a six-hour settlement negotiation. I was the newest attorney on the team and felt proud to have been invited. After we settled, the partner I worked for had publicly praised the talking points I'd prepared.

When I got to the subway, the platform was already packed. For a moment I thought about trying to get a cab, but Christopher and I had dinner reservations. I figured the subway would be faster. A bad decision.

Inside the car, overheated bodies pressed against me on all sides. The new birth control pills I'd recently started taking made me run hot. My neck and my armpits were damp with sweat. On top of that, my too-high and too-pointy stilettos pinched my toes. I cursed myself for not changing into the white Reeboks stuffed into the bottom of my tote bag. Another bad decision, one driven solely by vanity. I hated the way the sneakers looked with the knee-length skirts my firm insisted its female attorneys wear. In truth, although I carried my sneakers with me everywhere, they spent more time in my bag than on my feet. At least, I thought as the door opened a third time and another crush of people fought their way inside, I'd been smart enough to take off my winter coat and suit jacket on the platform, stuffing both into the oversized tote.

Somewhere between Twenty-Third Street and Fourteenth Street, the train lurched and jolted to a stop. A woman standing nearby crashed against me. The lights blinked on and off, then the car went dark.

"What the fuck?" a man with a heavy New York accent yelled.

"Not again," another woman standing a few feet away muttered. "This is the second time today."

Shit, I thought. Spring Street was my stop. From there it was a few blocks to the Soho loft I still shared with Christopher. So close, and now stuck. All around me people grumbled. They sounded annoyed and angry, but no one sounded afraid. Although I continued to be afraid of sleeping alone, standing in the crowded subway car my biggest fear was that a pickpocket might reach into my bag and steal my wallet or keys. Instinctively, I took one hand off the pole and checked to make sure my tote bag was zipped. After a few minutes, the grumbling stopped. The train grew silent except for the scuffing of shifting shoes and the occasional cough or sneeze.

I don't remember how long we'd been stalled when I felt a large hand with thick fingers on me. My silk tank top fell loosely around my body, leaving room for the hand to creep inside. It grabbed my breast and squeezed tight. I screamed—although my scream must have sounded more like a yelp or a gasp. The hand pulled away. No one else moved. And then, almost as if it were timed, the lights blinked on and the train jerked to a start.

As my eyes adjusted to the light, I scanned the faces of the men on the car. There were dozens of them: clean-faced men in suits, acne-covered teenagers in leather jackets, and a homeless

such a pretty picture

guy dressed in layers of coats. I searched for a satisfied smirk, for a furtive glance at the floor, but they all looked guilty to me.

No one had touched me without my consent since I was fourteen. I tried to breathe. Just a squeeze on the train, I told myself, a New York City subway incident. Most of my friends had similar stories to tell. The year before, a guy had jerked off on Sarai, ruining her favorite winter coat. In comparison, this episode was nothing. I tried to stay calm, but my body refused. By the time the train pulled into the Fourteenth Street station, my legs were shaking. When the subway stopped, I pushed my way out, knocking into a teenage girl in a plaid kilt and knee socks.

Ignoring the gelatinous feeling in my legs, I ran up the stairs onto the street without stopping. Outside, Fourteenth Street thronged with people. I walked fast, my high heels clicking purposefully on the sidewalk: past the discount stores lining Fourteenth; past the men standing behind tables, beckoning people to purchase fake Louis Vuitton purses and Cartier watches; past the people rushing to and from the subway. Latin music and hip-hop blasted from dueling boom boxes, taxis honked, and the ever-present sound of sirens shrieked in the distance. I had been living in Manhattan for eight years and the sounds of the city were white noise to me. But that day, the noise throbbed in my head and pulsed in my eardrums. I wanted to make it stop.

I kept walking. Numb to everything but the noise, I walked for blocks until my legs shook so badly I had to stop. At Union Square, I found an empty bench across from the Coffee House, a popular restaurant with a good bar where Christopher and I occasionally went with friends for drinks. I worried that someone I knew might see me. I was in no shape to pretend to make idle chitchat. As the afternoon light faded, I stared into space. Thinking about the hand, I had an overwhelming urge to cut myself, something I hadn't done since college. The thought was too much to bear. I put my elbows on my knees, my face between my hands, and began to cry.

I sat on the bench, hunched and crying, until I felt a tap on my shoulder. Shrieking, I jumped up and found myself face-to-face with a gray-haired woman in a tan trench coat. In one hand she carried a bulging leather briefcase.

"I didn't mean to scare you, dear," she said.

Still dazed, I looked around. The sky had turned black, and the unseasonable spring weather had blown away, leaving winter in its place. My shoulders felt stiff from hunching over. I stretched my neck and twisted my head from side to side.

"Are you all right?" she asked.

"I'm fine, just stiff."

"I heard you crying," the woman persisted. We were standing near a streetlight, and I could see that her eyes were blue. Her voice sounded concerned, but her eyes looked hard and more than a little judgmental.

I smoothed the wrinkles out of my skirt and ran my fingers through my hair. "I'm fine," I repeated. "I had an argument with my boyfriend." I still had my jacket off and rubbed my arms to get warm, but my hands felt like icicles.

"Did he hurt you? Hit you?" I locked eyes with her. Definitely judgmental. I flashed on an image of my mother and shuddered.

"No, nothing like that. I overreacted." I opened my tote bag and pulled out my coat. "I should be getting home."

The woman stood watching me as I slipped on my coat and picked up my bags.

"Thank you." I turned to walk away, but she touched my arm.

"I have a daughter about your age. You need to be more careful. This city is dangerous."

I thought about walking home, but my body felt tired and bruised, as if I had been in a physical fight. It was over a mile to the apartment, so I decided to hail a taxi. Well past rush hour, the street was flush with empty cabs, and two raced toward me the moment I stuck my hand out. As I climbed inside and settled against the cracked leather seat, I inhaled deeply and let myself relax for the first time in hours, grateful to feel safe.

Christopher opened the door to our apartment before I could put my key into the lock. "Where were you? It's after seven." He tapped his thick gold Rolex. "We missed our reservation."

We'd been together for over fourteen months. A time frame that was close to my breaking-up point and, I had learned, his. Although I had not known it when we moved in together, Christopher, who was five years older than I was, also had a history of short-term serial monogamy.

"The meeting ran long and then the train broke down."

"Your mascara is smeared," he said with an edge of impatience. "You look like Tammy Faye Bakker." He moved out of the way and let me into the apartment. "Were you out with your friends?"

In the taxi on the way home, I had contemplated telling Christopher what had happened on the subway, but I was afraid that he would judge me for taking my jacket off. All of my life people had told me I was too sexy and that if I wasn't careful, men would think I was looking for trouble. *No, it was better not to tell*, I thought.

"Don't be ridiculous," I said instead, "I was working. I'm tired, I just want to take a shower."

When I got out of the shower, I readied myself for an impending fight. But by the time I had dried my hair, Christopher had ordered Chinese food. For the rest of the evening, we sat on our couch—eating dumplings and fried rice out of white cartons and sharing a bottle of Beaujolais.

Andrea Leeb

"I'm sorry I didn't call before I left the meeting." The lie had become a truth to me. I stabbed a dumpling with a chopstick and popped it in my mouth.

"I'm sorry too." Christopher reached over and wiped a dribble of soy sauce off my chin. "My temper. I get so jealous."

I put a finger to his lips. "It's all fine. Let's forget about it."

chapter 31

I did my best to hold it together, ignoring my lack of focus at work, the missed steps in aerobics classes, and the momentary feelings of breathlessness that came and went without warning. *Don't dwell on it*, I said to myself every morning. But at some point each day, my mind would flash on the hand, then on the boys in the woods, and then finally on my father, the bath, and everything that came after. No matter how hard I tried I could no longer remember how to forget.

Two weeks after the incident, as I stood in line in a crowded deli, I felt a pain above my heart. Not a twinge, but a sharp agonizing pain like an icicle plunging deep under my skin. Instinctively, I touched my chest with my hand. When I pulled it away, I half expected to see blood.

"I have to get out of here," I mumbled, pushing my way past the office workers waiting for their sandwiches or salads.

Stumbling onto the sidewalk, I stuck my hand out to wave a taxi down. The pain radiated from my chest to the tips of my fingers. A heart attack. I thought I was going to pass out in the middle of Park Avenue.

Clutching my chest, I climbed into the cab. "New York Hospital Emergency Room," I gasped.

The cabbie turned around and stared at me through the plexiglass barrier. "Lady, you should be calling an ambulance," he said in a thick Bronx accent.

Andrea Leeb

I wiped the beads of sweat off my brow as the icicle plunged deeper. "I'm fine. Just drive."

"You better not fucking die in my cab." He blew his horn and merged with the uptown traffic.

They admitted me quickly. A doctor with a neat black bun and wire-frame glasses examined me. "Probably anxiety. You're young for a heart attack, but we can't take any chances."

Alone in a small cubicle separated from other patients, I lay on a stretcher, waiting for the test results. Dressed in a hospital gown and covered only by a thin sheet, I shivered from the cold. I had an IV in my left hand and a heart monitor attached to my chest. I could tell from the steady rhythm of the beeping machine that I was physically okay, but they hadn't given me anything for the all-consuming pain. I moaned and took a deep breath of the Lysol-scented air. The icicle plunged deeper and I moaned again. I wanted Christopher to hold me. I wondered if the doctor had called him like I'd asked her to.

I lay in pain for an hour, trying to distract myself by counting the number of carts and gurneys I heard rolling past my cubicle.

A nurse in blue scrubs entered my room. "The doctor said your tests were normal." She pulled a syringe out of her pocket. "Valium. It will make you feel better."

I tasted the medicine as it hit my veins. A few minutes later, the icicle in my chest began to melt.

The doctor came into my cubicle after another thirty minutes or so. "As I thought, a panic attack." She stood with her hands in her pockets and her stethoscope around her neck. The expression on her face let me know I'd wasted her time with my neurosis. "We called your boyfriend. Twice. Once he gets here, you can go home. You need to follow up with a therapist. The nurse will give you a referral list."

such a pretty picture

By the time Christopher showed up it was after five o'clock. *Of course he waited until the market closed*, I thought as the curtain parted and he stepped inside. Pulling the curtains shut, he stared at me without saying a word. Dressed in a navy double-breasted suit, his black cashmere coat draped over one arm, I felt his eyes taking in my hospital gown, the IV in my hand, and my sweat-matted hair. *Not so perfect now*, I thought.

"The doctor said you had a panic attack."

"I'm sorry." I pulled the sheet up to my chin.

He shook his head. "Honey, I don't know what's going on with you, but this isn't what I signed up for."

An hour later, we sat across from each other at the kitchen table. Christopher had ordered pizza and opened a bottle of wine.

"You haven't touched your food," he said.

Lubricated from the wine and the remnants of the Valium, I felt like I could breathe again, but my mouth tasted like metal from the IV. "I'm not as hungry as I thought I was."

"You're never hungry lately," Christopher said. "You're losing weight."

"You know what they say: You can never be too thin."

Christopher shook his head. "Honey, you need to tell me what's going on."

"I thought you didn't sign up for this." The moment the words left my mouth, I wished I could take them back.

Christopher's eyes flashed. I waited for the mean comment, but it didn't come.

"Seeing you in the hospital freaked me out." He stood up and walked around the table, stopping next to my chair. "It was a stupid thing to say."

Grabbing my hand, he pulled me up next to him. I didn't resist. He kissed me once and then guided me toward the living room couch.

"Tell me," he said after we'd sat down. "I promise whatever it is, I won't get angry."

I wasn't sure I believed him, but I needed to tell him something. Despite my misgivings, I began to talk. I told him about the boys in the woods and about the subway. I told him that since the subway, I had begun to unravel. My voice shook while I talked. I didn't tell him about the party, the one that had ruined my thirteen-year-old reputation. And most importantly, I didn't tell him about my father. Although I hated to admit it, the stigma of incest had profoundly colored my life. I was afraid that Christopher would think I was dirty and that my part, regardless of my innocence, was unforgiveable. Deep inside, I was ashamed of myself, and I didn't want the man I loved to be ashamed of me too. Our relationship was far from perfect, but I wasn't ready to lose him.

"I hate seeing you like this." Christopher took my hand. "Why don't you take a day off from work? I'll treat you to a spa day at the Red Door. A full day of pampering will make you feel a lot better."

"Thank you, you're probably right." I leaned over and gave his cheek a peck. I just wanted to end the conversation, although I knew full well a spa day wasn't going to fix me.

chapter 32

I'd scheduled my first appointment with Hope for late in the afternoon. I'd called her because she was one of two women on the referral list of therapists and because, alphabetically, her name came first. As I walked up the street to the building, I noticed a thin ray of sunshine from the last light of the day hitting the parked cars—silver, blue, and red metal sparkling under a lavender sky. It reminded me of a rainbow, and I felt optimistic.

Walking into Hope's office, my optimism faded. The waiting room was windowless with barely enough space for a tired green couch and a coffee table. The walls were bare and the wooden floors stained and uneven. What kind of therapist rents an office like this?

"Andrea?" A woman who appeared to be in her mid-thirties opened the door. She had auburn Botticelli curls and wore an orange sweater and brown skirt with matching tights. She reminded me of a sunny fall day. "I'm Hope," she said, and motioned me into the inner office.

I thought about how much I hated the idea of therapy. *I should leave*, I said to myself, *give her a check and go.*

The inside office looked as dingy as the waiting room and was even smaller, with only enough room for an office chair and a love seat. I imagined Christopher's distaste for this shabby little office and this woman and her autumn clothing. *Can't you find someone more high-end?*

"You told me on the telephone you're having problems with your boyfriend. Is that what brings you here?" Hope asked once I got settled.

"I'm not sure," I said, comparing Hope's brown tights and sensible block-heeled loafers with my own designer pumps and sheer stockings.

"What aren't you sure of?"

Without responding, I contemplated the woman in front of me. Her features were pleasant—just short of pretty. On her left hand she wore a simple gold wedding band. Her skirt fell below her knees; her sweater was baggy and shapeless. I wondered if she were Orthodox, but she wasn't wearing a wig. No, not Orthodox, just not consumed by her appearance. I studied my manicured hands without speaking. How was I going to explain myself to this woman? I couldn't imagine her carelessly riding the subway in a loose silk tank top or see her as a young girl ending up in the woods with three boys she didn't know. I couldn't even begin to think about her ever letting her father touch her or causing her mother to go blind. Would she judge me? Would she tell me I should have been more careful? That everything that had happened was my fault?

"Andrea?"

I looked into her eyes. They were wide and light brown—the color of almonds.

Something about her gaze seemed empathetic and a little bit sad, as if she understood my pain all too well.

"It's complicated."

"If it were simple, you wouldn't be here."

On that first visit I surprised myself. Maybe it was because of the sadness I saw or imagined in Hope's eyes. Maybe talking to Christopher had prepared me, like a dress rehearsal. Or maybe I was just desperate. I told her about the subway and about the boys in the woods. I didn't tell her about my father. I wasn't ready. At the time, I didn't think I would ever be.

such a pretty picture

"I don't understand why I'm so upset," I said at the end of the session. "The boys were a long time ago, and the subway was a boob grab. I shouldn't have been riding around dressed like that. Why can't I forget about it and move on?"

"You were touched without consent," Hope said. "Assaulted. You have every right to be upset."

chapter 33

"Christopher and I stopped having sex," I said. "He hasn't shown any interest since I told him about the boys and the subway."

I sat in Hope's office on her faded green couch. For the past three weeks, I'd been seeing her twice a week. I'd come directly from work, dressed in my lawyer's uniform: a navy suit with lightly padded shoulders, a pale blue silk blouse, and matching suede stilettos. I had taken off my winter coat, but I kept it and my briefcase next to me. I always wanted the option to leave quickly.

"How does that make you feel?" Hope asked. She sat across from me dressed in what I'd already come to think of as her therapist uniform: an oversized sweater, olive that day, dark skirt, tights and loafers.

I picked at my already chipped red nail polish and torn cuticles.

"Andrea?"

"A little rejected and a lot relieved."

"Relieved?"

"There are times when the best thing about being in a relationship is having someone next to me in the bed. It makes me feel safe." Although I had known this about myself for years, I had never verbalized it to anyone else.

"You used the word *safe*," Hope said. "Can you tell me more about that?"

such a pretty picture

Shit. Why had I brought up sex? I picked up my coat and slipped it back on.

"Are you cold?" Hope asked. "Uncomfortable?"

I stared at her, deciding whether to stay or leave.

"Sex is hard for me." I wished the office had a window so I could stare at the city or at anything besides Hope's kind face.

"It's common with survivors of sexual assault."

I grimaced. I hated the word *survivor*. It made me feel like a patient or worse a victim. "In the beginning having sex was hard."

"With Christopher?"

"I meant the very beginning, with my first boyfriend, Brian," I said. Closing my eyes, I began to talk. I told her about Brian, our summer kissing on the rocks and listening to David Bowie. I spoke without stopping. Describing in detail the first time we tried to have sex, I told her how I couldn't let him in. "We tried several times," I said. "But I couldn't. He broke up with me over the phone."

"Brian was a little shit," Hope said.

I shook my head. "He was seventeen."

"You mentioned that when you were trying to have sex, you saw your father's face. You said you smelled him."

Fuck. I took a breath. I had been so involved with the story, I had slipped. "I didn't say anything about my father. You must have misheard me."

"I didn't mishear." Hope met my eyes. "But we don't have to talk about it now."

I checked my watch. She had let me talk ten minutes beyond our time.

"It's late. Christopher is waiting for me."

When I got home, the apartment was dark. I flipped on the lights and walked into the kitchen. The answering machine on the counter blinked red. One new message at six p.m.: "Going to Pete Lueger's for dinner and then drinks with the boys. Home around ten. Love you." Early in our relationship, this late notice would have annoyed me. But that night I felt grateful. A respite from choking down dinner and pretending to be okay.

Shaken by memories, I took a small paring knife out of the drawer and walked into the bathroom. Stripping off my clothes, I climbed into the shower and ran the water, leaving the knife at the edge of the tub. I had trained myself to stop cutting during my junior year of college. That year, I had my first real boyfriend after Brian. That boy was the only one who ever asked about my cuts. When I told him they were cat scratches, he had lifted an eyebrow. "Must be one big cat." Afraid of more questions, I vowed to stop. The first few weeks, I felt like a junkie going through withdrawal. I shook each time I put down the razor blade, the scissors or the knife, but the value of appearing to be normal was worth more to me than the pain. Since the subway incident, the repressed urge to cut had returned.

I turned off the water and picked up the knife. As I pulled back the shower curtain, I saw my reflection in the bathroom mirror: my wet hair, my naked breasts, my throat, my mouth, my eyes. Dark and narrow, they were identical to my father's eyes. Sometimes it hurt to look at them. Staring into the mirror, I put the knife against my chest and cut.

chapter 34

My relationship with Christopher continued to deteriorate. We were more like roommates than lovers. He never even noticed the cut on my chest. Over the next month, I continued to see Hope twice a week. In our sessions I told her more about the boys in the woods, the subway, and my relationship with Christopher. But I still didn't talk about the things that I needed to talk about most: my father's abuse and my mother's complicity.

I knew the time had come to tell. That nothing would change without telling the truth. But I couldn't. Every time I tried, my mouth went dry. Like a person having an allergic reaction, my throat closed and the truth remained unsaid. I was reminded of how similar I was to my mother. She could see no evil and I could speak no evil. In the end, I must have said enough, because Hope brought the subject up to me.

"Andrea, have you ever heard of repressed memory syndrome?" she asked.

I clenched my teeth and stared at her.

"Andrea?" Hope asked me again, followed by, "Does my question make you uncomfortable?"

All of your questions make me uncomfortable, I wanted to scream. "I've read about recovered memories."

As I understood it, there was a school of thought in psychology that said that victims of trauma like rape or incest subconsciously blocked their memories as a way to protect themselves. It was controversial. A lot of psychologists and psychiatrists didn't believe it was real. In the early 1990s, repressed and, especially, recovered incest memory was in the zeitgeist. The internet was not yet in the mainstream and cable news was almost nonexistent, but there were articles in multiple magazines ranging from *People* to *Time*. The high-profile survivors included celebrities, daughters of millionaires, and even a Miss America. A year or so later, some would recant and say they were confused. Others would stand by their stories.

"Is it possible . . ." Hope began to ask, but I interrupted her before she could finish.

"My memories are not repressed." I sat with legs crossed, my upper leg swinging back and forth. I felt the familiar itch in my throat and tightness in my chest.

"Sometimes memories are lost or blocked. It's nothing to be ashamed of."

I shook my head. She hadn't understood me. My memories were not lost or blocked. They were consciously buried in the vain hope that someday I would forget them.

"My father molested me!" I yelled, and instantly regretted it. I covered my mouth with one of my hands. "I'm sorry," I mumbled through my fingers.

"Oh, Andrea," Hope said. "You have nothing to apologize for."

Over the next three sessions, I told her the story. I began with the bath and my mother's hysterical blindness. "Before he took her to the hospital, he even dressed her up like she was going to a party. Nobody asked any questions. Not that night and not later."

With each session, I went further, describing the years that followed and my mother's refusal to see the abuse that went on in front of her. Once I started talking, something inside of me

such a pretty picture

shifted. My subconscious mind became like an underwater volcano slowly breaching the surface. Every secret I shared brought me closer to eruption. By the end of the third session, I became obsessed with confronting my parents.

Hope shook her head. "It's too soon. You may not get what you want. We need to make sure you're ready, to come up with a plan so you can protect yourself."

Before I left I promised I'd wait.

chapter 35

On Saturday mornings, Christopher played racquetball. I usually went to the gym at the same time, but that Saturday I stayed home. It had been only three days since I'd made my promise to Hope. Intellectually, I knew she was right, but the little girl in the bathtub had waited long enough. I told myself I could handle it. I told myself I would be fine.

I decided to make my calls in the bedroom, locking the door behind me just in case Christopher unexpectedly came home early. Knowing my throat would get dry, I put a glass of water on my nightstand. I opened the blinds and stood in front of the window. A sunny day, I watched people walking outside. Some of them carried brown bags filled with freshly baked bagels from the deli around the corner. Others held bouquets of flowers wrapped in newspaper or strolled down the street empty-handed. I glanced at the alarm clock: nine o'clock. I still had time to make my usual nine thirty step class. I could talk to Hope on Tuesday and together we'd come up with a plan. Dismissing these thoughts, I sat down on the bed and picked up the phone.

I started with Sarai. As I dialed her number, I prayed she wouldn't be home. In the chaos of our childhood, we'd shared almost everything, but I still hadn't told her about the way our father had touched me. Listening to the phone ring, my stomach clenched. She picked up.

such a pretty picture

"Dad touched me when I was younger," I said, not able to say the words *abuse*, *molestation*, or, worst of all, *incest* to my sister.

"Touched?"

"Sexually." I swallowed hard and waited for her to respond.

"Are you sure?"

I exhaled. "I'm sure."

"When did it start?"

"I was four and a half, when Mom went blind." Sarai had been too young to remember our mother's blindness, but she'd heard at least part of the story.

"Did she see it? Did she know?"

"She had to know. I was in seventh grade by the time he stopped."

"But Dad doesn't like children," Sarai said. "Pedophiles love children."

Pedophile. I had never used that word to describe my father. Hearing it made me nauseous. I felt an urge to defend him, to tell her it was complicated, that it wasn't his fault. "I don't think he did it because he liked me."

"Why didn't you tell me this before?" Her voice quivered.

I coughed and took a sip of water. "I didn't tell anyone. I thought it was my fault. I didn't think anyone would believe me. Did he . . . ?"

"No. He hit me, but he didn't do *that*."

Before we got off the phone, she asked me one more time if I was sure. When I said yes, she didn't respond. The silence between us killed me.

"I believe you," she said after five long seconds, "but I can't hear any more about this. It's just too much for me."

After we hung up, I sat clutching a pillow to my chest. The sun streamed into the room and I began to cry. I thought about my sister and my father. She had a girlhood filled with bad memories, and I'd just given her one more. I wanted to call her back.

I wanted to tell her he's not that bad. *Remember the petting zoo*, I wanted to say, *how he rescued you from the goats*.

I didn't call her back. I knew she needed time. I'd been wrong to tell her over the phone, but I'd been too scared to tell her in person. Later, after she had time to digest the news, we'd talk about it more. In my father's harem, we'd each had our role. Sarai had her own secrets: not sexual abuse, but far more hitting than I'd been aware of. Or perhaps, like my mother, more hitting than I'd allowed myself to see.

My mother answered the phone. "What's up, glamour-puss?"

Her voice sounded cheerful, and my eyes filled with tears. "Mom. There is something I need to tell you." My breath caught in my throat and I coughed.

"Are you getting sick? You need to take better care of yourself. You work too hard."

"Dad molested me," I said. I had meant to ease into it, but the ability to ease was beyond me.

"Nonsense," she interrupted before I could say more. "I will not listen to lies about your father." Then she hung up.

I'd expected her to deny it, but not to hang up on me. My hands shook as I put the receiver back on the base, and I knocked the glass of water off the bedside table. I didn't move to retrieve it or mop up the water. About five minutes later, the phone rang. My parents were both on the line.

"We can't believe you're doing this to us," my mother said. I heard the anger in her voice. It stung my body like lightning passing through the telephone wires.

My father, on the other hand, sounded preternaturally calm. "I'll take a lie detector test," he said. "I'll send you the results."

"David, you don't need to do that." My mother paused. "This whole thing is a fairy tale. Your father did not do what you are accusing him of."

such a pretty picture

"What about the bath? Your blindness?"

"That's what this is about?" she asked. "You already know the story. I went blind because I was worried about you. When I walked into the bathroom and saw that your father was bathing you in cold water, I went ballistic." My mother's voice broke. "My reaction wasn't your father's fault. You can't blame your father for my blindness."

"There were other times," I persisted.

"Stop it!" she shouted, and then paused again. For a few seconds, we sat in silence. I could almost hear her thinking. "Don Green," my mother said. "He was in and out of the house all the time."

Don Green was one of my father's friends. As far as I knew, my parents had not seen him for over twenty-five years.

"Don and Daddy looked like twins. Everyone said so. They even wore the same black-frame glasses." My mother's voice sounded relieved. "He was a real sicko. Do you know, he once suggested we do a couple's swap? His wife was so ugly, I thought your father would pass out. Remember that, David?"

My father didn't respond but my mother continued, reeling off a list of Don Green's purported perversities. As I listened to her craft her new reality, I lifted outside of my body. I saw myself sitting on the bed, pressing the phone against my ear, but I couldn't focus on what she was saying. I didn't know it then, but the story that she came up with that day would be one she'd maintain for decades. It was, I'd realize later, the best she could do.

My father finally spoke. "Ange, I'm sorry you're confused. We should have gotten you more help when you were younger."

chapter 36

I am standing in a glassy bay. The water is bathtub-warm and hits my knees. Tiny fish circle my ankles, their silvery scales glittering in sunlight. Out of nowhere, the water recedes and the placid ocean turns from aqua to black. A towering wave rises, churning its way toward me. There is no time to run. The wave hits like a wall. Cold and dark, it sweeps me under, flooding my lungs with salt water and sand. Fighting against the force of the water, I desperately try to breach the surface. I want to live.

I hadn't had a tidal wave dream since my father stopped abusing me. But after the phone calls, they returned. At first, a couple of times a week, and then nightly. I woke up sweating and screaming, my muscles stiff and sore. I'd have to pinch myself to be certain the dreams weren't real.

During that time, my lifelong ability to compartmentalize disappeared. The terror of my nightmares became my metaphorical reality. One moment, I'd be writing a brief, my head bent over my computer, a stack of legal books at my side. The next, I'd be gasping for air, swimming toward a surface that was no longer there. Each day that passed, the moments of terror came more often and with less warning.

At home, Christopher was no longer angry, just confused. And I was afraid. Afraid of losing my job, my boyfriend and my

such a pretty picture

home, but mostly afraid that I no longer had the strength to fight the wave churning inside of me. I remembered the night on Key Bridge and the siren call of the dark water. Plunging. Filling. Soothing. An end to the shame and the pain that came with it.

Afraid, I talked with Hope about going to an inpatient program or a hospital. I knew better than to bring up suicide, so I told her I needed a break. It took several sessions. I'd bring it up, waffle, and then bring it up again. We discussed different programs and hospitals. There was a psychiatric hospital in the Midwest with a program specializing in treating survivors of sexual assault.

"It's the best one, but you'd have to commit to a minimum of six weeks." Hope handed me a brochure.

"Six weeks is too long," I said, and gave her a list of excuses. I didn't have enough vacation time; it was too expensive; Christopher would be upset if I left for so long. All of the excuses had a grain of truth, but there was a bigger truth: I was afraid that if I went away for that long, I'd never make it back. I'd become a permanent patient. As I talked to Hope, I pictured myself in ten years. Wrapped in a flannel bathrobe, padded slippers on my feet, my face bloated from medication and my hair tangled, I saw my future self shuffle mindlessly down an endless linoleum hallway. It might have been irrational, but to me that was scarier than suicide. I'd rather jump.

The program we found was at a rehab for drug and alcohol addiction.

"They have a related program for trauma survivors," Hope explained. "It's men and women, and not directed solely to sexual assault, but I'm sure there will be others who've had similar experiences. It's not my first choice for you, but it's only twelve days."

"Twelve days sounds good." Just enough time to regain my equilibrium. A quick fix.

Andrea Leeb

❦ ❦ ❦

The rehab running the program was located in a rural community about four hours outside of the city. The person who took my information over the phone told me there were two buses every day. "We are only a few miles from the bus station," she said, and gave me the number for the local taxi company.

I had planned to take the bus. Ashamed of my weakness, the idea of getting there on my own made me feel like I was still strong enough to take care of myself. But when Christopher insisted on driving me, I agreed without hesitation.

On a gray Saturday morning in mid-May, I stood in the parking garage and watched Christopher put my small suitcase in the almost equally small storage space under the hood of his pristine silver Porsche. We were both dressed in blue jeans, expensive cowboy boots (the soles of which had never seen a field, not to mention a horse), and black leather jackets. We looked like a typical yuppie couple going away for the weekend, but we climbed into the car without speaking. As we pulled out of the garage it began to drizzle. I was already jumpy, and the rain exacerbated my nerves. Christopher would be driving more than eight hours to make the round trip. If he had an accident, I would never forgive myself.

As we drove through the tunnel under the river, Christopher took one hand off the steering wheel and placed it on mine. "Are you sure you want to do this?"

"I have to." I turned away and focused on the white tiles of the tunnel wall.

"Can't you just take a couple of weeks off and see Hope for extra sessions?"

I turned and faced him. He looked so sad. This step was too much for him. "It's less than two weeks," I said. "I promise everything will be fine."

such a pretty picture

The drive was long and boring: concrete and cars. The rain continued and we drove most of the way without talking. When we finally got off the turnpike, the landscape changed. Instead of concrete, we were surrounded by trees and lush green pastures lined with purple and yellow flowers.

As we drove we passed through a quaint colonial town. It reminded me of New Hope and, for a moment, I imagined a weekend at a bed and breakfast. I saw the two of us holding hands while we visited charming shops and took strolls on rolling country roads. We could return home on Sunday afternoon and go back to our life the way it was before the subway, before Hope, and before the phone call with my parents. We'd write off the whole episode. It wouldn't be perfect, but it would be good enough. Then I thought again about the dark water and the churning wave. There was no going back.

A white sign marked the entrance to the rehab grounds. We followed a long road until we reached a building made of stone, and behind it several small houses. It reminded me of a boarding school or an upscale summer camp. The person I had given my information to over the telephone had instructed me to look for a white clapboard house with a large porch. "There'll be a sign and arrows. It's the only twelve-day program we have right now. Everyone else will be in the main building."

When we pulled up, two men were sitting in rocking chairs on the porch. One had short dark hair, and the other one was blond with longer, curlier hair. They both wore blue jeans and flannel shirts and looked to be in their early forties. They must have been talking before we arrived, but as our car hummed to a stop they just looked at us.

"What are those freaks staring at?" Christopher asked.

"Probably the car. I don't think they have many Porsches out here."

"Those guys look strange."

I shook my head. Christopher had been upset when I told him there would be men at the program, but I'd thought we'd gotten past it. "They're harmless," I said.

He touched my hand. "You don't need to do this."

Please don't make this harder, I thought. Opening the car door, I stepped onto the gravel driveway and walked up the first two steps of the porch.

"Is this the right building for the adult trauma program?" I asked, although I knew the answer. I smiled, trying to convey that I was friendly and not the stuck-up city bitch that I looked like.

"Through the door and make a right for registration," the blond man answered. For a moment, our eyes met. His were a pale blue. A beautiful color, but they looked tired and sad. *Weeping eyes*, I thought, although there were no tears I could see.

"Honey," I heard Christopher say. I turned and walked back down the steps. He had popped open the hood of the car, but left my suitcase inside. When I reached him, he put his arms around me. "Come home," he whispered, pressing me against his chest.

"Let's take a walk." Grabbing his hand, I pulled him to the end of the driveway out of earshot of the men on the porch.

The sun had finally broken through in patches. We leaned against a fence that faced an empty green field. Droplets of water sparkled on the individual blades of grass like tiny diamonds. We talked for a half hour. Everything we talked about had been said before.

"I need to do this," I said over and over, not sure who I was trying to convince.

By the time we walked back, the two men had left. Christopher took my suitcase out of the car and brought it up to the top of the porch for me.

"I don't understand you," he said.

I hugged him. His eyes glistened as if he were holding back tears.

such a pretty picture

"I should go," he said. "I have a long drive." He turned and walked back down the stairs.

Standing on the porch, I watched him climb into his car and drive away, the roar of the Porsche's motor shattering the quiet countryside.

chapter 37

When I asked the teenaged girl at the reception desk for my room key, she told me the rooms had no locks on the doors. "For safety." She gave me a gummy smile. I thought about arguing, but she seemed so young she reminded me of a candy striper. I decided I'd speak with someone with more authority later.

My room looked like a college dorm room, small with a twin bed, a nightstand, a dresser, a small wooden desk and a chair. I'd paid extra for a single.

I had been inside for only a few minutes when someone knocked on my door. "Hello, may I come in?" came a woman's voice.

I opened the door to find a freckle-faced young woman dressed in jeans and a smock top with pockets. She looked older than the girl at the desk but not by much, maybe twenty-six at most. She had an ID badge fastened to her smock, and in one hand she held a clipboard.

"I'm Jenna, one of the junior counselors."

I smiled and motioned her inside. "How can I help you?" I asked, thinking I could talk to her about changing rooms. There had to be at least one room with a door that locked.

"I need to check your bags."

"Excuse me?"

"Your bags? The girl at admissions was supposed to do it, but she forgot. She's new."

such a pretty picture

Admissions. The word sounded strange. "You want to search my bags?"

"It's routine," Jenna said. "We check everyone's bags. For drugs, alcohol, and instruments of self-harm. You know."

I shook my head. "No, I don't know." I sighed. First no locks, and now this invasion of my privacy.

"Would you mind opening it for me?" Jenna pointed to my suitcase, which I'd put on the edge of my bed along with my handbag. "I'll need to look in your purse too."

Rolling my eyes, I opened my handbag and then unzipped my suitcase. "Search away," I said, not bothering to hide the annoyance in my voice.

"It's nothing personal." Jenna put her clipboard down and pulled a pair of latex gloves out of her pocket.

She started with my purse. My handbags were notoriously messy, the one place I expressed my inner chaos. I was glad I'd cleaned out that particular purse the night before. She opened my wallet. Taking out each of my credit cards, she stuck her index finger into the little slots. She looked in the billfold, pulling out the cash and counting it. Four hundred dollars, my getaway money.

"You weren't supposed to bring a lot of cash or valuables."

I stared at her without responding. I was paying to be at this place.

"If this were the rehab program, we'd have to hold it for you."

"But this is not the rehab program." I put my hands on my hips. My head throbbed. I should get the fuck out of here fast.

"No, it's not." Jenna stuck the money back into my wallet. "If the money gets stolen, it's your responsibility."

She opened my makeup bag next, and took out my mascara, blush, and the small bottle of foundation I kept inside. She opened each one without saying a word until she got to my lipstick.

"Lancôme," she said, and took off the cap. "I love this red."

I fought the urge to tell her that with her coloring she shouldn't even think about wearing it.

After she finished with my purse, she turned to my suitcase. One by one, she unfolded my T-shirts, my extra pair of jeans, and my running shorts. She stuck a gloved hand inside the pockets of my jeans. Then she took out my bras and panties, fourteen pairs stuffed into a Ziplock bag. She dumped the underwear on the bed and rifled through the lacy, extra-small thongs—as if I could hide anything inside of them.

Watching her touch my clothing made me feel like a criminal. My chest tightened and I felt dizzy. Right then it hit me that despite the quaint buildings, the woods and wildflowers, I was in a mental hospital. They might call it a program or rehab but, regardless of the name, I had checked myself into a place where people had to be protected—from themselves and from each other. I had voluntarily walked into my worst nightmare.

"Breathe," I murmured to myself, and sat down on the other side of the bed. *Do not have a panic attack in front of this kid.*

"Are you all right?" Jenna tilted her head to one side. She reminded me of an errant puppy. I could tell she didn't mean any harm, but I had not expected to be searched.

"I'm fine," I snapped. "Please finish this up so I can unpack."

"Really, this is nothing personal."

"It is completely personal," I said, as she took my running shoes out of a larger plastic bag.

Without answering, she shook them, looking at the floor as if she were expecting drugs to come tumbling out.

"What's this?" Jenna pulled a small iron out of my suitcase.

"A travel iron."

"You don't need this here."

My chest tightened again. "I always travel with it. Everywhere." A true statement. I'd backpacked through Europe, Egypt, and parts of Central America with my iron in tow.

such a pretty picture

"I have to take it."

"I'm compulsive about wrinkles." I heard the edge of panic in my voice. I thought about offering her my red lipstick as a bribe. "I'll be really careful."

Jenna scribbled something on her clipboard. "Can you please sign and initial?" She handed the clipboard to me. "You'll get it back on discharge."

Admissions. Discharge. The tightness in my chest turned to pain; my fingertips felt numb. I needed to get out of there. I looked at my watch. Six o'clock. Too late to catch a bus back to the city. I'd have to wait until morning.

"Tomorrow's schedule." Jenna pulled a yellow mimeographed sheet out of her pocket. "Dinner is right now. Tonight, it's optional, but for the rest of the time, attendance at meals is mandatory." She smiled at me and gave me a little wave. After she closed the door behind her, I crumpled the paper into a ball and tossed it into the wastebasket.

In for the night, I slipped into my sweatpants and began to build a barricade. I would have built one even if the room had had a lock, but without one it felt urgent. First, I tried to move the nightstand, but it wouldn't budge. The desk chair would have to do. I wedged it under the doorknob. Then, except for the clothes I'd laid out for the morning, I repacked my suitcase and put it in front of the chair. It was not enough to keep someone out, but at least it would give me time to scream if anyone tried to come in.

chapter 38

At three thirty in the morning, I gave up on sleep. Before going to bed, I had spread my clothes out on the desk. I ran my hand over my black T-shirt, attempting to smooth out any wrinkles. Keeping an eye on the door, I dressed quickly. I'd seen a pay phone on the first floor, but it was too early to call a taxi. I'd wait another half hour. Once home, I'd tell Christopher he was right: A spa day and a little shopping would solve all my problems. I'd tell Sarai I'd made a mistake, apologize to my parents, assure my father that he didn't need to take a lie detector test. I'd stop going to therapy, and put the subway incident and everything else back into the black box I stored in the recesses of my mind. I had done it before; I could do it again. Lying down on the bed, I closed my eyes. A half hour, I told myself.

Rolling my bag behind me, I walk through a white door into a wooden shack. It changes from a building and then into a shack again. Inside, a single large room with rows of empty benches. The benches look like they should be in a church, not a bus station. The walls are painted a dark gray. I spot the ticket window in the corner of one wall. A man sits inside wearing a green visor, small round glasses, and black suspenders. He looks like something out of a Dickens novel.

such a pretty picture

"May I help you?" He flashes me a gold-toothed smile.

"One way to New York City."

"One dollar."

"One dollar?" I think I misheard him, but he smiles at me with his gold teeth and nods. I open my wallet and search for a one-dollar bill. Confetti paper flies into the air like tiny moths. I can only find a twenty, and I don't want to ask this odd little man for change. I check my pockets and finally find a dollar bill.

I sit on the bench alone with my ticket in my lap. Waiting. Except for the man with gold teeth, I am the only person in the bus station. The door at the front of the terminal opens. A man in a beige trench coat walks inside. His features are blurry, but he has black curly hair and he is wearing thick-framed black glasses. As he walks closer, his face comes into focus. My father, but not my father now. My young father. He looks like he did at twenty-seven. How can my father be younger than me? I am not sure it's really him. Then he smiles, and I see the slanted chip in his front tooth.

"I'm glad to see you've changed your mind about all of this," he says, and bends down to kiss me.

"No!" I woke up screaming. I didn't know where I was. I took in the room: my suitcase and my boots, the desk chair jammed under the doorknob. I checked my watch: eight forty-five. I'd missed the early bus, but if I left now I'd be home by dinnertime. I pulled on my boots and began to dismantle my barricade. As I pushed my suitcase away from the door, I remembered the dream. I saw my father's smile as he bent to kiss me. I put my arm to my nose and inhaled. I could smell the scent of him on my skin, as if it were permanently tattooed into my senses. I took the crumpled sheet out of the trash can. Group Therapy in fifteen minutes. *One day*, I thought. *I'll give it one day.*

Andrea Leeb

⚐ ⚐ ⚐

Five minutes later, I walked into a large room with brown wall-to-wall carpeting. Two women and a man sat together on metal folding chairs. The man was tall, with short dark hair. I recognized him as one of the men who'd been sitting on the porch when Christopher and I arrived. One of the women was dressed in jeans and had spiky blonde hair. Although we couldn't smoke inside, she had an unlit cigarette in her mouth. The other woman, dressed in slacks and a sweater, gave off an aura of professionalism. A red lanyard with an ID card dangled from her neck. Seeing me, she stood up and walked over.

"I'm Laurie, the senior therapist. You must be Andrea."

"How did you know?"

"I met everyone else at breakfast."

A red-haired woman in oversized pink glasses and a rail-thin girl who looked like a teenager but who, I'd later learn, was in her mid-twenties walked into the room. They were followed by the blond, blue-eyed man from the porch and another, younger man with a crew cut and tortoise-shell glasses.

Laurie turned to greet them. "Take a chair and make a circle." She gestured to a stack of chairs against the wall. "There's fresh coffee on the table by the door." Then she directed her attention back to me. "We were talking about breakfast?"

"I'm sorry, I overslept." I flushed, feeling like a bad teenager.

"Grab a seat and a cup of coffee. There's sugar and nondairy creamer. If you want real milk, you need to come to breakfast."

I shot her a fake smile. "I take mine black."

Seven of us were enrolled in the program: three other women and three men. The spiky blonde was Donna, the redhead with big glasses, Mary, and the thin one, Jennifer. The blond man from the porch was Bob, the tall, dark-haired one, Jacob, and the younger man with the tortoise-shell glasses, Shaun.

such a pretty picture

After introductions, Laurie gave us our schedule: large group therapy daily; small group (same-sex) therapy four times a week; individual therapy twice a week; and one consultation with the facility psychiatrist. Then she moved on to the rules, a notebook full of them.

"It's important to respect each other's boundaries. Romantic relationships are prohibited." She paused for effect before continuing to read. "During your free time you can walk the grounds, meditate, or write in your journals." When she was done, she closed the notebook, put it back on the floor, and picked up the pile of composition books at her feet.

"Speaking of journals," she said, the tone of her voice growing warmer. "I have one for each of you. We will be giving you daily assignments."

She had to be kidding. I averted my eyes and stared at the carpet. It was worn down to the weave in spots. It made me think about Hope's office and how she'd wanted me to go to a different program. Maybe I should have listened. Then again, it could have been worse.

We spent the next two hours talking. "Sharing," Laurie called it, using a vernacular of group therapy I wasn't yet familiar with. One by one, she asked each of us to talk. Over the years, I'd lost my childhood need to disappear among strangers. My shyness had been completely eradicated by law school and the practice of law. But that day, as the others spoke, I shifted in my seat and ripped at my cuticles. Except for telling them my name and that I lived in New York, I didn't say a word. Unlike everyone else in the program, I'd never been in group therapy or any kind of twelve-step meeting. I felt unsure about what to say or not say, especially around men.

The stories the others told were heartbreaking: children hit with belts, with boards, thrown down stairs, left alone in cars for hours while parents drank or drugged. Broken arms and legs.

Andrea Leeb

Refrigerators filled with vodka but empty of food. Nauseating, endless abuse. Shaun, with the tortoise-shell glasses, lost his sight in one eye from his father's punch. Listening, I compared. My life had been privileged. I had never been hungry, never sent to foster care. Materially, I'd had everything. The worst place I had lived in was the Bucks County Motel, and that was for less than a year. Yes, I'd grown up in a violent, chaotic home. Yes, dishware and furniture were thrown. But no bones were broken; Sarai and I had beautiful clothes, books, toys, and pets. As long as you didn't peek behind the closed bedroom doors, compared to the others my childhood seemed normal, even good.

chapter 39

I stood facing the beige wall and pressed the receiver to my ear. The pay phone was located in a hallway right outside the kitchen. The smell of the overcooked pot roast we'd had for dinner lingered in the air.

"It's me," I said to Christopher when he picked up.

A Tuesday night, our first phone call since I'd checked in on Saturday. Over the past few days, we'd left messages, him with the front desk, me on our answering machine. But we kept missing each other.

"I guess they keep you guys busy," Christopher said now.

"Therapy. Hours and hours of therapy."

"Right, therapy. I've been thinking about that since I dropped you off."

"I miss you."

"You don't belong there."

"Christopher . . ."

"Let me talk. That place is filled with weirdos."

"You don't know that."

"I saw them. Honey, you're a lawyer."

I sighed. Appearances were important to Christopher. He loved my pedigree: my law degree and the white-shoe law firm with the fancy name where I worked.

"Christopher, they're nice people."

"You put yourself into a mental hospital."

"It's a program, not a mental hospital," I said, although I was not completely convinced he was wrong. I still questioned whether I belonged or even deserved to be there.

"It's a mental hospital. You aren't crazy."

"Please stop." In my group, we had finished our third day of therapy. I sat through all of it, hardly speaking and without shedding a single tear. But as I listened to Christopher, I began to cry.

"That place is going to mess you up."

"Mess me up or mess us up?" I heard footsteps coming down the hall. Bob, the blond-haired man, was walking toward me. Seeing me on the phone, he stopped, but he must have noticed my tears. "Are you all right?" he mouthed.

I nodded and gave him an okay sign.

"I'm worried about you," Christopher said.

"Don't be." I was still crying. I watched Bob walk back to the end of the hall just as Shaun and Donna rounded the corner. The house had only the one pay phone; after dinner, everyone wanted to use it. Giving me my privacy, Bob turned his back to me and gestured to the others. They made a line, facing away from me. Embarrassed, I squatted against the wall, cupping my hand over the receiver.

"Come home," Christopher said. "I'll take the day off and come get you tomorrow."

"I can't," I said, ignoring the fact that I had been on the fence for days. "There's something I need to work out."

"The subway was bullshit, and those boys a long time ago. Let it go."

"I don't think I can." I wondered what he'd say if I told him the truth about my father.

"You know, you sound worse, not better."

"Please understand," I pleaded.

"I have to go." He hung up without telling me he loved me.

I slid the rest of the way down to the floor. The receiver dangled in front of me. As the busy signal began to beep, my quiet

such a pretty picture

tears turned to hiccupping sobs. Years later, I would think about this call and about Christopher. At the time, I viewed him as unsupportive and angry. While this perception may have been true to me, it was also true that I was never completely honest with him. I just assumed that he was not equipped to handle my past. I never gave our relationship, or any of my prior relationships, a fair chance.

On Wednesday, the day after my call with Christopher, I shared in both group therapy sessions for the first time. Until then, I'd said little, acting more like an observer than a participant. My meltdown by the telephone had made it clear to me (as if it were ever in doubt) that I belonged here. After I'd delayed their evening phone calls, I felt like I owed it to the group to say something.

That day, I talked about my father's temper, his drinking, the broken glass, tipped tables, and the constant fear of an imminent storm. I talked about the good things too: pretty dresses, bicycles, and the leather-bound books that had saved me from total isolation. I felt relieved when no one told me I was too privileged or that the pain I felt was unearned, mitigated by my middle-class upbringing.

I spoke as honestly as I could, without telling the whole truth. I wanted to but I couldn't. The sentences eluded me. I dreaded the words that I knew I would have to say: incest, molestation, perversion, pedophilia. Filthy, shameful words. Even worse than the words, I dreaded the questions: Why did you allow it? Why did you let it go on so long? Why didn't you tell someone? And the worst question of all: Why didn't your mother stop it?

On Thursday, the sixth evening, I went to my room after dinner. It had been two days since my call with Christopher. We hadn't talked since, although I had left a message on our answering machine. I sat down at the desk in my room and stared at the journal I'd been given on the first day. I was supposed to write in it each night, but I had resisted. Except for briefs, memos, and law review articles, I had not written a word, not even a personal letter, since I was fourteen.

That year, I'd sent one of my Emily stories to a friend of my father's. An editor at a publishing house, he'd taken the time to read it and had even written me back. "*Your writing is good but the story feels forced. The protagonist's family is too perfect, like* Leave It to Beaver. *Writers need to be honest. Write what you know.*" Reading his response, I imagined the horror on his face if I had written about the family I knew. If honesty was what I needed, then writing was a pointless goal. I took my pink diary and composition books down to the basement and put them into a cardboard box. When a burst water pipe destroyed the box and everything in it during my junior year of college, I didn't give it a second thought.

Now, as I sat at my desk fingering the smoothness of the composition book, I wondered if it was time to write again. Earlier in the day, I'd had my individual therapy session with Laurie. We'd sat in her office on the first floor, both of us in overstuffed blue corduroy chairs. She had a big window and the curtains were partially open. Outside, Bob, Donna, and Jacob—the smokers—gathered under an umbrella.

"In group you're still keeping secrets." Laurie sat with her legs crossed yoga style. "Pretending."

"Pretending?" I asked.

"That your father didn't sexually abuse you."

I was barefoot, having slipped off my flip-flops. I pulled my legs up onto the chair and hugged my knees against my chest. "I'm trying."

"Are you?"

such a pretty picture

My mother had taught me that if I were smart enough and pretty enough, I could trick myself into believing that none of the bad things had ever happened. "It's so hard," I replied.

"If you can't talk about it and you can't journal about it, try writing a letter. Read it aloud to the group. Then throw it away."

"Share with everyone?" I hugged my knees tighter. "All six of them?"

"Isn't that why you're here, to stop keeping secrets?"

Cracking the journal open, I stared at the blank pages. It had been raining nonstop for days. That night, the rain grew stronger. Hard, torrential drops pounded the roof. We had no TV or newspapers, but earlier that day the girl at the desk had told me the rain was finally going to stop in the morning. "At least you guys will have six days of sun," she'd said. Six days out of twelve, halfway through the program. *Was Laurie right? Had I come here to stop keeping secrets? Or for something else?* I didn't know. But whatever it was I wanted, I was running out of time to get it. Picking up my pen, I wrote my name on the inside cover of the journal and began to write.

I skipped the salutation. "*You offered to take a lie detector test,*" I wrote, "*but we both know you never will. It doesn't matter anyway. I don't need a lie detector test to remind me of the truth. I remember because, no matter how much I try, I can't forget. You changed my life forever with a bath . . .*" I wrote about the bath, the bicycle, and the years of abuse that followed—a recitation of harm and confusion. "*You must've thought the price for my silence came cheaply, but the cost to me cannot be calculated. You poisoned me with your touch. You damaged me for life and expected me to go on as if nothing had happened. Branded me with a secret. Now all these years later, I don't know how to love. I don't know how to live. There are times when I am not sure I can.*"

I wrote to my mother too. I told her I kept my father's secret to protect her: from the truth and from the public shaming she might endure if I ever divulged it. I told her that I wanted her to love me. I wanted her to see me, to believe me, to forgive me, to let me forgive her and to help me forgive myself. "*Despite it all I love you, and I know that in your own way, you love me too.*"

Many hours later, I heard an alarm clock buzz on the other side of the wall, the sound of a door opening and closing. It was already morning. I had fallen asleep at my desk, but before I did, I had written twelve rambling pages—some of it illegible, all of it painful.

"*I will not deny the truth any longer,*" I wrote to both of my parents. "*I don't know what this means for our relationship. But I must be honest with myself. My life depends on it.*"

I sat in the circle with my journal on my lap. I stuttered as I read the words I had written. I read like I wrote, in a dissociative blur. I don't remember when I began to cry, only that I did.

"You can let go of it now," Laurie said.

Everyone watched silently as I stood up and walked to the trash can. One by one, I tore out the pages and ripped them into a thousand pieces. A symbolic goodbye to a secret no longer hidden.

As I made my way back to my seat, I noticed Mary and Jennifer crying.

"Can we hug you?" Mary asked.

I nodded yes and opened my arms wide enough so Donna could join too. The men stayed put, watching. For that I felt grateful. When I sat back down, Jacob, the dark-haired man, was looking at me.

"I have two daughters," he said, shaking his head. "I'm so sorry."

"That letter must have been difficult to write," Laurie said to me.

I sighed and closed my eyes.

such a pretty picture

"Not as difficult as living it," Bob said.
I opened my eyes and met his.
"Living it was harder," I agreed. "Much harder."

chapter 40

After the group session, I needed to be alone. Behind our house, there were three gravel paths that someone had long ago carved into the surrounding woods. I chose one randomly.

The rain had finally stopped. Sunlight streamed through the trees, but the air still felt thick and moist. The only sounds I heard came from birds and squirrels rustling through tree branches and the soles of my cowboy boots crunching the gravel. I stopped walking after a few minutes and stood in the path, listening to the silence. After so many years of living in New York City, I missed the quiet of the countryside. Inhaling the pungent smell of damp wood and soil, I closed my eyes and tried to empty my mind.

Walking again, I focused on the path in front of me instead of the morning behind me. Since the rain had stopped, the day grew hotter by the minute. Still wearing the jeans and the black T-shirt I'd worn to therapy, I began to sweat. I had thought about changing into shorts before I left our building, but I already felt vulnerable. Better to stay covered.

I had been walking for about ten minutes when I heard footsteps behind me. I picked up my pace, but the footsteps picked up too.

"Andrea." A man called my name.

I turned and saw Bob jogging toward me.

"Do you want some company?"

such a pretty picture

I didn't, but I thought it would be rude to say so. "Of course," I said with what I hoped was an authentic smile.

We walked for about twenty minutes before we came upon a playground. It sat alone in the middle of a small grove of pine trees. Two old swings, a sandbox filled with pine needles, a rusted slide, and a rotting wooden plank that must have once been a seesaw. Somebody's childhood abandoned and decaying in the middle of nowhere.

"Who would put a playground here?" I asked.

Bob pointed at the ground, which like the sandbox, was carpeted with pine needles. "Whoever it was lost interest. Nobody's set foot on this place in years."

"Do you think we're still on the rehab's property?" I wondered if he had been there before. If he had seen me take this particular path, knowing if he followed me, we'd end up here. I eyeballed him. He was not as tall as Christopher, maybe five foot ten, but he had at least six inches on me. Dressed in jeans and a flannel shirt with the sleeves cut off, he looked sinewy and strong. He reminded me of an older version of one of the boys who'd assaulted me in high school. I studied his face, his blond hair and his pale blue eyes. Despite the heat, I shivered.

"I think so." He pulled a pack of Marlboros out of his shirt pocket and offered it to me. I didn't smoke, at least not regularly, but I took one. "You were fearless today." He handed me a disposable lighter.

I didn't want to talk about the session or my letter. I lit my cigarette, inhaling slowly until the tip glowed orange. I felt the smoke burn my throat and travel into my lungs. That first inhale was the best part of smoking. I exhaled and handed the lighter back to him.

"How did you get to keep a lighter when I couldn't keep my travel iron?"

"Your what?"

"A miniature iron. They confiscated it. I have to go to the office to iron my clothes."

"You brought an iron here?" He laughed.

"I hate wrinkles. Why does everyone think that's so strange?" I shook my head. "I still can't believe they took it from me."

Bob smiled. He had a gap between his front teeth, but they were straight and surprisingly white for a smoker. "Ya got to know how to stash the contraband."

"I should've met you earlier." I took another puff of the cigarette.

"I don't think your boyfriend with the fancy car would've been too cool with that."

Remembering that day, I frowned. Christopher had called Bob a freak when we'd pulled up. He'd glared at him when I got out of the car. I'd hoped Bob hadn't noticed, but of course he had.

"He's worried about me."

"He looked more angry than worried." Bob took a hit off of his cigarette and exhaled.

"He didn't want me to come here."

"Truth is, he should be worried about you."

I took a step back. "Why would you say that?"

I looked around. There was nothing and no one in sight. Our building, all the buildings, were at least a mile away—too far for anyone to hear me scream. Our group had been living in a bubble of intimacy for six days. But in reality, Bob was a stranger. I ran through a list of facts I knew about him. He lived in Virginia with his fiancée—they were planning to get married in the fall. Twelve years sober, he worked as a drug counselor in a rehab. His fiancée was pregnant, and he'd come to this program to learn how to be a better father, to break the chain. His own father, an alcoholic, had hit him "like a punching bag" until Bob left home at sixteen. A deposition list of facts, none of which made him either dangerous or safe. In the end, all that mattered was that he was a man, and I was a woman. For a moment, I felt flooded with a familiar self-hatred. How fucking stupid could I be? Thirty-three years old, and I still couldn't find the line where safety ended and danger began.

"We should go back." My voice cracked.

"I didn't mean to scare you. It's just that you've been through a lot. Anybody who loves you should be worried."

"Christopher doesn't really know what I've been through."

"How could he, if you don't tell him?" He took another hit off his cigarette. "There's something I want to tell you. Something I've never told anyone. Not my therapist, not even my fiancée."

His eyes were moist with tears. He stood chewing on his upper lip. He felt so familiar, but it wasn't the blue-eyed boy from the woods that he reminded me of after all. It was someone else. I tried to figure it out, but I came up blank.

"Why tell me?" I kicked the pine needles away to make a clean patch of dirt and then threw my cigarette down, grinding it out with the tip of my boot.

"Because of your letter. Because you'll understand."

"We can talk on our way back." Bending down, I picked up the cigarette butt and started to stick it into the front pocket of my jeans.

"Don't do that." He pulled a plastic baggie out of his back pocket. There were already a couple cigarette butts inside. He held it out in front of me. "Put it in here. The smell of a half-smoked cigarette is a lot worse than a couple of wrinkles."

Looking at him holding the open baggie, my body softened. I smiled in spite of myself.

We each sat on a swing. His legs were stretched out in front of him like a giant child. He reminded me of Tom Hanks in *Big*, an eleven-year-old boy trapped in a man's body. His jeans had pulled up past his ankles, and his white socks peeked out of his paint-splattered construction boots. I remembered he'd mentioned he worked as a house painter on his days off.

He took the pack of cigarettes out of his pocket and studied it as if there were something new or interesting written on the front. His hands shook.

"When I was eighteen, I went to prison."

"Prison?"

"For pot. I was dealing. Mostly nickel and dime bags, sometimes an ounce."

He held the pack of cigarettes out to me. I shook my head no. "You really went to prison for selling nickel bags of pot?" In college, I'd known lots of kids who'd been small-time dealers. A couple of them had been arrested, but nobody I knew ended up in prison.

"It was 1968, in Virginia. Dirt-poor rednecks like me went to prison for selling pot. Rednecks and Blacks."

"Eighteen is so young."

"Eighteen is older than five."

I gasped. "I wasn't in prison."

"Really?" He arched an eyebrow.

He told me he'd pled guilty. His public defender had assured him he'd get a reduced sentence.

"Bad advice, or bad luck with the judge," he said. "Four years straight to prison. I'd been playing guitar in a bar band. I had hair halfway down my back. I shaved it in jail. I'd hoped it would make me look tougher, but it only made me look younger."

I imagined an eighteen-year-old Bob in an orange jumpsuit and leg shackles, his blond curls shaved short enough to see his pink scalp, his face still unlined and innocent. He must have been so frightened.

He knew people who had been inside. They'd warned him. The best way to avoid getting raped on your first night was to burn your mattress and get locked in solitary.

"More bad advice." He laughed a nervous laugh.

They locked him in solitary just like he'd been told, but as soon as they'd changed from evening to night shift, the guards opened the door of his cell. Three prisoners walked in, men old enough to be his father. "Probably the same age I am now," he said. Two held him down while the other one raped him. One after another. The guards walked away, closing the door behind them. Nobody heard him scream, or if they did, nobody cared.

"Oh my God." It hurt to look at him. I stared at the ground and pushed the swing back with one of my legs. The rusty chains creaked, and I started to cry.

"The shame is crippling. Still." Tears ran down his face. "Sometimes I feel like I'll never really be free."

Our eyes locked. "I know," I whispered.

I wanted more than anything to hug him, to hold him against me and rock him like a child. I wanted to promise him that he would be all right—that we both would. But there were boundaries we could not cross, and promises I knew better than to make.

"I was so fucking naive; I actually thought those guards would protect me."

"No one protected you." I pictured him, the men, and the guards. And then I pictured my mother. My chest tightened. I tried to take a breath, but the air felt like mud. I heard the buzzing of bees. Growing lightheaded, I wrapped my hands around the link chains on each side of the swing so I wouldn't fall.

"Are you okay?" I heard the tears in his voice.

I nodded. *He knows*, I thought. *He is me.* For a moment I could feel our bodies touching, as if the chains were gone and the empty space between us had closed. As if we were one.

"Me neither," I said. "No one protected me either."

We sat on those children's swings for over an hour. Two broken adults, each of us crying for ourselves and for each other. Grieving for the children we had been, and the adults we had become. Neither of us said a word until pink filaments of evening threaded through the sky.

Andrea Leeb

"We should go back now," Bob said. He stretched his body upright.

I stood. Two large birds circled above us. From a distance they looked majestic, but I had long ago learned that everything looked better far away.

"Do you think they're hawks or vultures?" I pointed to them, hoping he would tell me they were hawks.

"Eagles," he said. "Let's call them eagles."

chapter 41

That night after dinner, I went straight to my room. Too exhausted to think about the letter or my conversation with Bob on the swings, I passed out. A few hours later, I woke up in a pool of sweat. I tried to recall my dream, but I couldn't. Instead, an image of an old photograph popped into my head. In the picture, my mother, her hair bleached platinum blonde and wrapped in a milkmaid braid, held a six-month-old me in her arms. Both of us were dressed in white and smiling. Her smile was uncharacteristically relaxed, and mine, toothless.

My mother had not been the type to fill our house with personal photographs. Growing up, we never took a family photo, and school pictures of Sarai and me were admired for a few days and then relegated to cardboard boxes. Through most of my childhood, our walls were sterile, and except for a few figurines—mostly on her dresser—our furniture was clutter-free. Later, after my parents settled into the house in New Hope and my father made more money from consulting, my mother began to cover the walls with paintings and to decorate tabletops and mantels with small bronze statues and cloisonné. But never a photograph. From my mother's perspective, it made sense. Without documentation, the past could be easily forgotten.

Andrea Leeb

The first time I saw the photograph of my mother and me, I was eleven. I'd been out of the hospital for only a week or so. My mother and I were home alone. We lay together on my parents' bed, intermittently reading and napping. The sheets were clean and wrinkle-free; they smelled like the spray-on starch my mother used to iron. I'd been sleeping there all week—anxious to watch my breathing, my mother had insisted. She'd banished my father to the foldout couch in his den. For once he'd complied.

"Is that me?" I asked, my eyes falling on the unfamiliar photograph. It sat on the top of her dresser, in a silver frame.

"You and me." My mother got up and brought the photograph to the bed for me to look at.

"I was such a fat baby."

"A beautiful baby."

In the photograph, my mother sat on an Adirondack chair with me on her lap. A posed picture in a dandelion-freckled field of grass.

"Where was this taken?" I asked.

"We were at Copper Beach in Westchester, visiting my parents at their summer bungalow." Her eyes were still on the picture. "Nanny and I found it in a box when you were in the hospital. Such a pretty picture. I'd forgotten all about it."

We sat for a few moments, both leaning against pillows, our shoulders touching as we studied the image.

"Those first couple of years after you were born were the happiest of my life. I loved you so much." My mother stroked my cheek. Her hand felt like silk against my skin.

"Are you still happy?" I didn't want to ask if she loved me less now.

"Yes, of course I am," she said, "but it was pure joy then. You were my perfect baby."

I focused on the word *perfect*. I had not been perfect for a very long time.

such a pretty picture

"What was the worst time?" I wasn't sure what I was asking her. What I was expecting her to say. Her blindness? Seeing me in the bath with my father? That was my worst time.

"The past month. Watching you in that oxygen tent, struggling to breathe." My mother started to cry. "I thought I was going to lose you. My oldest baby. I couldn't bear the thought."

"I'm sorry." I put my head on her shoulder.

"Why are you sorry? I love you. You're home now. Safe with me."

My room at the rehab was on the top floor of the house. Above me, the patter of some kind of animal on the rooftop interrupted my memories. "Safe with me." I repeated the words that my mother had said to me over twenty years before. I turned on the bedstand light. Two a.m., my personal witching hour. Alone in my hot little room, I tossed in my bed. My nightgown stuck to my skin. I needed fresh air.

Tiptoeing, I crept into the hallway and down the stairs. The wooden stairs creaked with each step I took. Downstairs, I scanned the dark lobby; the night counselor was nowhere to be found. According to the rules, we were not allowed to leave the house after eleven p.m. Out the front window, a clear, half-moon night beckoned to me. If I got caught, I'd take the lecture in stride. With less than a week left and my breakthrough that morning, I doubted they'd expel me for sitting on the porch. The front door was closed but unlocked, and as I pushed it open, I stopped for moment, half expecting to hear an alarm. Nothing. So much for the rules. Anyone could have left or, worse yet, walked in and murdered us all. At least we were safe from careless ironing.

Outside, the air was clean and fresh from days of rain. I inhaled the faint scent of still-damp soil. Above me, a galaxy of stars glittered like silver sequins against a black velvet sky. Someone, maybe the night counselor, had left the porch light on, and a family of moths flew in and out of its glow. I sat on the top step, tucking my knees into my chest, and rocked my body like a little girl. Too early in the summer for the chorus of crickets or katydids, the night was silent. A cloud of bats circled the large oak tree directly across from the house. There must have been fifty of them. I closed my eyes. For a heartbeat, I thought I heard their wings flapping, but I must have imagined it.

Listening to the quiet, I thought about my mother. My father's crimes were unforgivable. But with my mother, it was more complicated. I could not comprehend her betrayal. I'd done so much to protect her, when she should have been protecting me. Most women would have left but she had stayed. And that hurt me almost as much as the abuse itself.

Was it hysterical blindness, or was she willfully blind? Either way, she sacrificed my childhood to keep my father happy. If I let her go, I would never have to see him again, have to hear him say my name or feel his eyes on my face and my body. But I couldn't do it. Even contemplating a life without my mother made my bones ache to the marrow. I wasn't ready to completely forgive her, and I knew I might never be. But I needed to give her the grace that she'd been unable to give me. If not for her, then for myself. I loved my mother. And despite everything, I couldn't bear the thought of living without her.

chapter 42

After the day at the swings, Bob and I spent most of our free time together. We talked about the people who'd hurt us, and the people we had hurt. I told him about Christopher, my ex-husbands, and all the other men in my life; the terror I suffered each night; and the coldness that enveloped me when anyone got too close. He told me about his fiancée and his girlfriends before her; the drugs and alcohol he had used to numb the pain; how he wanted to be a better man than his father. I don't know about Bob, but I'd never been that honest with anyone before, not even with a therapist.

As the emotional intimacy between us grew, the others in the program noticed it too. Conscious of the prohibition on romantic relationships, we were careful not to leave the house or the porch unless we were with a group. We never touched. It wasn't only the group or the rules we were afraid of; although we couldn't define it, our relationship transcended desire. Deeper than friendship, we had no name for it, but we both knew we had to be careful not to destroy it. For my part, I understood how easily I could turn any relationship with a man into something harmful and mean, and so I refrained. I wanted something more. Something to cherish. A model for future love.

Our last evening at the program, the two of us sat in rocking chairs on the porch. An almost full moon illuminated the trees. A still, windless night, the quiet broken only by the sound of our rockers creaking against the wooden slats. The program had ended right before dinner. We would both be leaving early the following morning.

"Eagles?" I pointed to the cloud of bats once again circling the large oak.

Bob leaned back in his rocker. "Night eagles."

"Two live in the portico in front of my parents' house," I said. "Every summer they hire someone to remove them, but they always come back."

"They hire a bat catcher?" Bob laughed.

"My father doesn't like to hurt living creatures. He won't even kill bugs."

"Your old man is one strange guy."

"An understatement."

"Have you made up your mind about confronting him again?"

I shook my head. "I'm not going to. I don't know what it would accomplish."

"No lie detector test?"

I laughed. It felt good to laugh about my father.

I studied Bob. "And you?"

"I'm going to tell Gail." He took a cigarette out of the pack he always kept in his front pocket. "It will help her understand."

"You will be a good husband and a good father."

He smiled at me. "I hope so," he said. "What about Christopher?"

I picked at my nails. Christopher and I had spoken twice over the last few days. We'd made up and professed our love, but he hadn't offered to pick me up and I hadn't asked. I would be taking the bus home in the morning.

"We may not stay together."

"Don't make any decisions about the relationship right away." He twirled the unlit cigarette between his fingers.

I nodded, although I had already made my decision to leave.

such a pretty picture

The bats were no longer in sight. I took a deep breath and held it for a second, then blew it out slowly. "I'm scared. I don't want to make my life about trauma. I don't want to be devoured by the past."

"We don't have to be devoured. But we have to be honest. We can't pretend bad shit didn't happen."

"Secrets are toxic," I chanted, repeating the therapy mantra.

He arched an eyebrow.

Closing my eyes, I rocked back and forth. I'd kept the secrets to stay safe, but instead I'd created a prison where I could no longer live. "How do I find it? That place between accepting and letting go?"

"You'll figure it out. I have faith in you." Bob stretched his arm in my direction, as if he were reaching to touch me.

We sat for another half hour before a few of the others joined us. With the larger group, our conversation turned to baseball, the beach, and the summer ahead. We were, we all agreed, ready to go home.

Before we went upstairs, Bob pulled me aside. "Don't read it until the bus," he said, and handed me a note. Written on journal paper, he'd folded it into a square.

"I don't have one for you." I had thought of writing him a note but decided against it, afraid of the words that might leak from my pen.

"I don't need a letter." He pointed to his chest. "I have this." He put his hands over his heart and bowed.

I never saw him again.

chapter 43

I took a taxi to the local bus station early the next morning. It was a single building with no magazine stand or vending machines, just a guy with a rolling cart who stood a few feet away from the ticket counter selling fried egg sandwiches and coffee.

On the bus, there could not have been more than fifteen other passengers, so I got two seats to myself. Everyone including me had bought a coffee or fried egg sandwich. The whole bus smelled like breakfast.

Although tempted, I had listened to Bob and not opened his note the night before. Instead, I had zipped it into the inside pocket of my purse. As soon as the bus rolled out into the street, I gave in. The paper was jagged on the side where it had been torn from his journal, his handwriting a clear cursive. I remembered he'd once told me that the only A he ever got in school was in handwriting.

Bob's note was only three sentences long. I ran my fingers over the words, picturing him hunched over the little desk in his room. I had never been close enough to Bob to smell his skin or clothing, but I'd always imagined his scent would be a mixture of tobacco and Ivory soap. Putting the paper to my nose, I inhaled. Nothing.

Words are not adequate to express what you have meant to me and how you have helped me. You are in my heart forever. Always have faith.

such a pretty picture

Reading the lines, my heart ached. I wondered what it would have been like if our lives had been different. Or if we had been reckless. Glad I'd waited to open the note until the distance between us was permanent, I reread it two more times before zipping it away.

Outside, the morning sky unexpectedly turned gray. Droplets of rain fell against the windows. At first it was falling lightly, but as we drove further east, the rain grew harder and the sky darker. "Who expected this?" I heard someone say. "The rainiest May I can remember," someone else responded.

I hadn't slept the night before. Listening to the steady patter of the rain, I covered myself with my jacket and closed my eyes.

I woke up a few hours later. The bus was more crowded, but not packed. Still raining, the wet highway glistened. The comforting smell of coffee had faded, replaced by an odor best described as rotting rubber. I pulled my jacket over my nose and fell back to sleep. About forty minutes later, I woke again, this time to the sound of the driver's voice announcing that we had reached the New York City Port Authority.

Stepping out of the bus terminal, the sounds of Eighth Avenue—honking horns, ambulances, footsteps on concrete—hit me like a wave. The Port Authority sat on the western precipice of Times Square, which at the time was still the home of pimps, porn, and peep shows. I stood frozen. People hurried in and out of the building. Across the street, a neon sign advertising SHOW GIRLS blinked red and white. Directly in front of me, a man in a Yankees cap stood behind a silver cart filled with boiling hot dogs. Next to him, another man, a Mets fan, sold hot pretzels. The aromas of steaming hot dogs, warm pretzels, and exhaust from the cars and buses mingled together to create a scent unique to the city.

Andrea Leeb

I walked to the taxi line at the far corner of the building. It was long, too long. The sky had lightened from gunmetal to powder gray, and the rain was now a drizzle, barely a mist. The summery air enveloped me. After I'd gotten off the bus, I'd packed my jacket into my bag. Now, with only my purse to carry and my small rolling suitcase, I decided to walk. I checked my watch, two o'clock. I pictured Christopher sitting in our apartment. Home from the racquet club, he was probably watching a Mets game or catching up on last week's *Wall Street Journal*. I hadn't called to tell him what time I'd be home, or that I'd arrived. Soho was almost two miles away, but I had time. I knew Christopher wouldn't start worrying for another few hours. A long walk would give me time to think, to prepare. All I needed to do was put one foot in front of the other and stay calm.

Making my way down Eighth Avenue, I stopped to buy a cheap umbrella. Just in case. At first, afraid a tsunami of panic would once again engulf me, I walked slowly. But after two or three blocks, I let the city's rhythm carry me. Some streets were empty, others more crowded. Everyone moved to their individual beat. My own steps grew steady, my pace measured. My body loosened and my chest opened. I could breathe. For the first time in a long time, I felt free. Emancipated from fear. As I walked, the sun cracked open the solid gray sky.

At the corner of Thirty-Eighth Street and Fifth Avenue, I stopped at the crosswalk next to a woman holding hands with a little girl. Mother and daughter. The little girl looked to be about four or five. She wore her hair in a single dark braid. As we waited for the light to change, her brown eyes met mine and she smiled.

Turning down Fifth Avenue, I thought about another dark-eyed girl. The one whose life had changed the night her father gave her a bath. In my mind, I saw her mother hand the girl to her father and walk out the door. I felt her father holding her close and pictured him lowering her into the tub. I shuddered. All

such a pretty picture

that girl wanted was her mother's love and her father's approval. Innocent and trusting, she needed someone to keep her safe. But nobody had, and nobody would. Not her mother, certainly not her father, not Dr. W or Dr. K, not Christopher or the men that came before him. Not even Bob. It was up to me.

I stopped and tilted my face toward the sky. Standing still, I let the afternoon sun wash over me with its warm golden light. Then I took a deep breath and started walking.

epilogue

When I left the rehab, I had hoped I was cured. I thought that by simply admitting the truth, I would wake up one sunny morning and find myself living a life filled with joy and free from shame. That perfect day never came. Although I no longer thought of suicide, the first several years were especially difficult; there were times when I felt as if I were stuck on a hamster wheel. Eventually, I realized that surviving incest is not tidy, and the decisions survivors make to survive are circular and filled with uncertainties. With time, I learned to be a little bit kinder to myself for any missteps or bad decisions (real or perceived) I made.

It wasn't easy, and there are still moments the shame rises and I struggle to find glimmers of joy. But those moments pass quickly, and today, living in the house I've shared with my husband for the past twenty-three years, I am happy. Strong-willed and resilient, I found a north star buried inside me. With time and therapy, I created a good life. I survived. No, more than survived. I thrived.

While I was still at the rehab, I made the decision to keep my mother in my life. This choice meant, by default, having a relationship with my father. It was hard. Sometimes I seethed and other times I disassociated completely. When he died, I felt only relief. Over the ensuing years many of my friends and even some therapists questioned my decision. Although I knew that other

such a pretty picture

choices might have been healthier, I never wavered or regretted my choice. My mother was my mother and, despite my anger, I loved her unconditionally.

In early April of 2023, my mother made the decision to stop taking the heart medications that had kept her alive. By then my father had been gone for six years, and my mother was living in a two-bedroom apartment with twenty-four-hour homecare. Recently retired, I temporarily moved in with her. "I'll stay until the end," I promised.

Two weeks before she died, my mother and I sat with our legs stretched out in front of us and our backs against plump pillows. The caregiver was running errands and except for Gizmo, my mother's Pomeranian, we were alone. Outside the sun shone brightly, but inside the curtains were drawn because the sunlight bothered my mother's eyes. The dark, hot room reminded me of a mausoleum. The only signs of life were the sweat pouring from my body and the sound of Gizmo's snoring at the foot of the bed.

"I have something I need to tell you," my mother said. "You have to promise me you won't cry."

I rubbed my mother's hand without answering. It was as small as a child's and her skin was onion-paper thin. I could feel her bones and her veins with the tips of my fingers. I turned my head so I could see her face.

"I was a terrible mother," she said, her eyes looking straight in front of her. She paused for a moment and turned her head toward me. Our eyes met. "I should have left your father." She started to cry.

I felt my eyes burning and swallowed hard. I had been protecting my mother since the day she went blind. I'd had decades of therapy, but there was still a kernel of guilt deep inside of me that blamed myself for her pain. Hearing her admission, my first urge was to tell her it was okay; I wanted to change the subject before she went any further. But I stayed quiet. She needed to talk and, more importantly, I needed to hear her. Not just the adult me, but all of us: the four-year-old me in the bathtub, the five-year-old me who taped her mouth and stuffed her nose with toilet paper in an effort to die, the fourteen-year-old me whose body looked like a map of razor-blade cuts and pinpricks, and every other iteration of me who had struggled with the pain of incest for the past sixty years. We had all waited a long time for this moment.

"I love you and I'm sorry," she said, her voice cracking. "I hope that someday you can forgive me."

My mother died at five forty in the morning on Mother's Day. Despite the morphine and the lorazepam, her death was not kind. Her chest rattled, and her once beautiful face turned masklike and grim. Holding her, I sang the songs she used to sing when I was very small, in the innocent days when we loved each other the most. The previous night my niece had brought over the book *Goodnight Moon*, and in that final hour I read it out loud. "Goodnight, Marlene, I love you," I told her. Dropping the book, I bent down and whispered into her ear. "I forgive you." As those words left my lips, my mother took her last breath and I forgave myself.

If you or someone you know has experienced sexual violence, *RAINN*'s National Sexual Assault Hotline offers free, confidential, 24/7 support to survivors and their loved ones in English and Spanish at: 800.656.HOPE (4673) and *Hotline.RAINN.org* and En Español *RAINN.org/es*.

Twenty-five percent of all royalties will be donated by the author to RAINN.

acknowledgments

It took me decades to garner the courage to write this memoir. I am eternally grateful to my sister, Sarai Leeb, for giving me her blessing and for reading it so many times. I know that revisiting our childhood was not easy.

Samantha Dunn, I wrote the first words and the last words of this memoir in your private workshop. Thank you for your ongoing support and friendship. I wish every writer could have such a warm and thoughtful mentor. Thanks to those early workshop readers who held my hand through those first painful chapters including Cheryl Jacobs, Jodi Forrester, and Mary Camarillo. A special thanks to my sister in spirit and writing, Catherine Cooper.

Thanks to Pam Houston—Pam, your guidance gave me the courage, the inspiration, and the strength to tell my story my way.

I wrote my first draft of *Such a Pretty Picture* in the Writing by Writers, DRAFT program, and workshopped a later draft at the Manuscript Bootcamp. To Samantha Dunn, Joshua Mohr, Pam Houston, and Karen Nelson, I am indebted to each of you. Ellie Rodgers, Elle Johnson, Catherine Cooper, Liz Tucker, Meri Johnston, Lynn O'Connor, Annie Lareau, Diz Warner, Quinn White, Anne Scott, and Anna Baker, thank you all for your careful reading and feedback.

Thank you to my teachers at the Bennington Writing Seminars. A heartfelt gratitude to fellow graduates Elizabeth Ziemska, Deborah Michel, and Karen Uhlmann. The three of you read multiple drafts and excerpts of this book. No matter how busy you were with your own work, each of you said yes, every time I asked. I am unbelievably lucky to have friends like you.

Thank you to Brooke Warner, Addison Gallegos, and the entire She Writes Press team for giving this book a home. And thank you to Jessie Glenn and the whole team at Mindbuck Media. I am fortunate to have many friends and readers, therapists, workshop leaders, and writers who supported me in writing this book. I appreciate your encouragement and kindness. Forgive me if I left anyone out.

Last, and most of all, thank you to my husband, Paul Balelo. I love you. Together we have built a calm, safe life. You help me to be a better person in every way. I am so grateful for your love.

about the author

Photo credit: Casey Pickard

Andrea Leeb is a writer and survivor advocate living in Venice Beach, California. She has an MFA from the Bennington Writing Seminars. Her work has been published in numerous literary journals, including *Litro Magazine*, the *Potomac Review*, *Text Power Telling* magazine, and *HerStry*. In 2025, she was a non-fiction finalist in the Tucson Literary Awards Program. Previously, Andrea worked as both an attorney and as a registered nurse. Currently, Andrea dedicates her time to writing, advocating for issues related to childhood sexual abuse and mentoring young women from post-conflict and climate-challenged countries.

Looking for your next great read?

We can help!

Visit www.shewritespress.com/next-read
or scan the QR code below for a list
of our recommended titles.

She Writes Press is an award-winning
independent publishing company founded to
serve women writers everywhere.